Praise for *Coaching A*

"The information age offers endless pos
organizations succeed. But we can never forget the ...
people and building a winning culture of communication, trust, and teamwork.
I appreciate the insights of *Coaching Athletes to Be Their Best*, and its focus on
the motivational power of a common purpose."
—Hall of Famer Joe Torre, four-time World Series champion manager
of the New York Yankees and MLB's Chief Baseball Officer

"This book provides a brilliant approach to relationship coaching that will
resonate with coaches and today's generation of athletes, allowing both to reach
new levels of performance and quality of experience."
—Kathy Delaney-Smith, all-time winningest Ivy League basketball coach,
Women's Basketball, Harvard University

"MI can enable coaches and psychologists to unlock the solutions that lie just
beneath the surface of everyday challenges. I highly recommend this book."
—Michael Gervais, PhD, sport psychologist; cofounder, Compete to Create

"Having spent 15 years as a college soccer coach, I can only imagine the type of
coach I could have been had I known about MI—and used it."
—Ben Freakley, MS, Head of Mental Performance, Toronto Blue Jays

"To help athletes reach their potential, I try to understand their personalities,
see what makes them tick, and ultimately find their 'drivers.' Using MI would
definitely help this process. Anyone who aspires to be as good a coach as he or
she can possibly be should read this book."
—Matthew Maynard, MBE, Head Coach,
Glamorgan County Cricket Club, United Kingdom

"Can conversations in sport get better? Yes, just like in all high-pressure working
environments, they can—with a strong foundation of care, trust, and more
skillful communication. This book has the potential to improve communication
between coaches and players, and to positively affect team culture."
—Imtiaz Ahmad, MD, Head of Medical Services,
Queens Park Rangers Football Club, United Kingdom

"The ideas, skills, and strategies presented in this book are so applicable in
everyday life that it would be easy to underestimate their transformative power.
The book is a treasure trove of interpersonal coaching skills. Emphasizing
affirmation over praise is just one example of a subtle change with potentially
revolutionary consequences. This book is essential reading for coaches, senior
leaders, and executives in sport."
—James Vaughan, MPhil, Head of Football and Coaching Psychology,
AIK Football Club, Sweden; cofounder, Player Development Project

"MI should be one of the first tools in the toolbox of the sport and exercise
psychology practitioner."   —Ian Maynard, PhD, CPsychol, FBPsS,
School of Sport, Rehabilitation and Exercise Science,
University of Essex, United Kingdom

"This book is a 'must have' for coaches in all sports. As a coach, I want to guide my athletes to greatness, and get frustrated when I am unable to effectively do so. This book provides insight and instruction on how to use MI to help my athletes determine their own course of action and become the performers they want to be."
—Matt Rhule, Head Football Coach,
Baylor University

"Motivation and behavior change are the core of what many of us in the sport and performance industry live and breathe every day. This book is a great resource for understanding MI as a tool to better understand and leverage athletes' own motivation to unlock their potential."
—Angus Mugford, PhD, CMPC,
Vice President of High Performance, Toronto Blue Jays

"Read this book and read it again. Fill it with notes in the margins and use it as a guide for 'being your best' as a coach. Your athletes will thank you for it!"
—Steve Rainbolt, Director of Track and Field
and Cross Country, Wichita State University

"MI has been a critical aspect of my sport psychology work for 15 years. Finally, there is a book specifically applying MI to sport, from an all-star group of authors. Straightforward enough for coaches to apply, yet nuanced enough for counseling professionals to learn from, this is a foundational book for the field."
—Mark Aoyagi, PhD, Professor and Director
of Sport and Performance Psychology, University of Denver

"If you are a coach of any kind, the strategies taught in this book will enable you to help your athletes help themselves. I will continue to refer to these tools to help me better serve the athletes I work with."
—Justin Su'a, MS, Mental Skills Coach, Tampa Bay Rays

"By building relationships, listening empathically, and meeting athletes where they are, the book shows how coaches can stoke the athlete's own internal fire to change. Ample scripts illustrate which communication strategies work, which don't work, and why."
—Deborah Roth Ledley, PhD,
private practice, Plymouth Meeting and Narberth, Pennsylvania

"Easy to read, with lots of real-life examples and practical suggestions for getting athletes to take ownership of their actions. If you want to have a positive impact on athletes, develop trusting relationships, and enhance motivation, then this book is for you."
—Robert Weinberg, PhD,
Department of Kinesiology and Health, Miami University

COACHING ATHLETES TO BE THEIR BEST

Applications of Motivational Interviewing

Stephen Rollnick, William R. Miller,
and Theresa B. Moyers, Series Editors

www.guilford.com/AMI

Since the publication of Miller and Rollnick's classic *Motivational Interviewing*, now in its third edition, MI has been widely adopted as a tool for facilitating change. This highly practical series includes general MI resources as well as books on specific clinical contexts, problems, and populations. Each volume presents powerful MI strategies that are grounded in research and illustrated with concrete, "how-to-do-it" examples.

Coaching Athletes to Be Their Best

Motivational Interviewing in Sports

Stephen Rollnick
Jonathan Fader
Jeff Breckon
Theresa B. Moyers

THE GUILFORD PRESS
New York   London

Copyright © 2020 The Guilford Press
A Division of Guilford Publications, Inc.
370 Seventh Avenue, Suite 1200, New York, NY 10001
www.guilford.com

Printed in the United States of America

This book is printed on acid-free paper.

Last digit is print number: 9   8   7   6   5   4   3   2

The authors have checked with sources believed to be reliable in their efforts to
provide information that is complete and generally in accord with the standards
of practice that are accepted at the time of publication. However, in view of the
possibility of human error or changes in behavioral, mental health, or medical
sciences, neither the authors, nor the editors and publisher, nor any other party who
has been involved in the preparation or publication of this work warrants that the
information contained herein is in every respect accurate or complete, and they are
not responsible for any errors or omissions or the results obtained from the use of
such information. Readers are encouraged to confirm the information contained in
this book with other sources.

Library of Congress Cataloging-in-Publication Data

Names: Rollnick, Stephen, 1952- author. | Fader, Jonathan S., author. |
  Breckon, Jeff, author. | Moyers, Theresa B., author. | Guilford Press
  (New York, N.Y.)
Title: Coaching athletes to be their best : motivational interviewing in
  sports / Stephen Rollnick, Jonathan Fader, Jeff Breckon, Theresa B.
  Moyers.
Description: New York : The Guilford Press, 2019. | Includes
  bibliographical references.
Identifiers: LCCN 2019031061 | ISBN 9781462541270 (Hardcover) | ISBN
  9781462541263 (Paperback)
Subjects: LCSH: Coaching (Athletics) | Motivational interviewing. |
  Motivation (Psychology) | Success.
Classification: LCC GV711 .R65 2019 | DDC 796.07/7—dc23
LC record available at https://lccn.loc.gov/2019031061

About the Authors

Stephen Rollnick, PhD, is Honorary Distinguished Professor in the School of Medicine, Cardiff University, Wales, United Kingdom. He is a cofounder of motivational interviewing (MI), with a career in clinical psychology and academia that has focused on how to improve conversations about change, and helped to create the Motivational Interviewing Network of Trainers (MINT; *www.motivationalinterviewing.org*). He has worked in diverse fields, with special interests in mental health and long-term health conditions like diabetes, heart disease, and HIV/AIDS. Dr. Rollnick has published widely in scientific journals and has written many books on helping people to change behavior. He is coauthor (with William R. Miller) of the classic work *Motivational Interviewing: Helping People Change,* now in its third edition. Dr. Rollnick has traveled worldwide to train practitioners in many settings and cultures, and now works as a trainer and consultant in health care and sports. His website is *www.stephenrollnick.com.*

Jonathan Fader, PhD, a clinical and performance psychologist, is cofounder of Union Square Practice, a mental health center, and SportStrata, a performance coaching group, both in New York City. He regularly works with professional athletes in Major League Baseball and the National Football League, and spent 11 combined years with the New York Mets and the New York Giants. Dr. Fader also works with performing artists, entrepreneurs, businesses, schools, health care professionals, and first responders, and speaks to groups on the topics of motivation, improving performance, stress reduction, improved communication, and team building. He is a member of MINT. His website is *www.jonathanfader.com.*

Jeff Breckon, PhD, is a Chartered Sport and Exercise Psychologist and member of MINT. Based in Sheffield, United Kingdom, he provides MI training to organizations across the United Kingdom, Europe, and North America; has published over 40 peer-reviewed articles; and presents internationally on the role of MI in sport, exercise, and health contexts. Dr. Breckon has worked clinically in sport and health contexts since 1992. His main area of interest is the role of MI in building a therapeutic alliance between practitioners and clients. He has played cricket in India and South Africa and played and coached volleyball and soccer in the United Kingdom and United States.

Theresa B. Moyers, PhD, is Associate Professor of Psychology at the University of New Mexico, where she conducts research on treatments for addictive behaviors, with a focus on MI. Her primary interests are identifying the active ingredients of MI as well as optimal methods for disseminating it in addictions settings. Dr. Moyers has published more than 35 peer-reviewed articles and has presented on MI and addictions treatment in 16 countries. She is a member of MINT. In addition to her academic pursuits, Dr. Moyers trains and competes with her border collie in the sport of dog agility. Her website is *www.theresamoyers.com.*

Preface

Relationships matter in sports, and we tend to navigate them through conversation. Everything you say has an impact, for better or worse. The spoken word is that powerful. How to harness the power of words to improve relationships and trust, and to have an impact on motivation and performance, is the aim of motivational interviewing (MI). If you, a coach, decide to do more than keep silent, the skills of MI can help you avoid stumbling or wasting your words.

This is the first book on MI in sports, and we use the word *coach* loosely to include all involved, whatever aspect of athlete performance and development you support—psychologists, managers, doctors, or specialists in fitness, nutrition, or performance, as well as parents. All it takes to begin with is curiosity about what you say to athletes and interest in how they respond. You might be good at tactics or managing people, or you might be more of a motivator and a people person; regardless, quality conversation can be added to your toolbox. We will hazard a guess that most of the conversation skills are already quite well developed within you. Our goal in this book is to help you refine them.

This author team lived in the parallel worlds of sports and counseling for many decades, as participants and psychologists in sports and as counselors in mental health. We cofounded MI for helping people forge new lives, and this approach was taken up worldwide by practitioners of all kinds, in hospitals, schools, clinics, prisons, interview rooms, and even on street corners.

The crossover of counseling work into sports turned out to be easier than we first thought it would be. We were all using MI quite naturally in sports, with individuals and in teams, focusing on anything from strategy to technique, recovery from injury, and well-being. What quickly became apparent to us was that in both counseling and sports, people do better when they feel trusted and encouraged to lift their motivation for themselves and make plans that they take ownership of. How to do this respectfully, efficiently, and effectively with athletes was the challenge.

What, then, is MI? It's a communication style with techniques that allow you to draw out the wisdom and answers from athletes (Miller & Rollnick, 2013). You will recognize it in what you already do, because it is based on well-established principles of good teaching, parenting, and coaching, in which a good relationship is central, where the learners or athletes are driving their own search for improvement, and where your expertise and advice are finely tuned to their needs. If you want to get better at harnessing the motivation within the athlete and handling those tricky everyday sporting conversations, then this book will help you do just that.

Does MI really work? One answer lies in the world of research, where we and others have evaluated the method in different settings, and where we have looked closely into the links among what you say, how you say it, and the outcome of your efforts. It makes a difference, and many hundreds of scientific trials bear this out. Another answer to this question is more immediate, in the reactions of the athletes we are speaking to. If they are energized by your conversation, then you know you are making a difference. MI is not a rigid recipe but rather a style and skill set for connecting with athletes and helping them thrive. Athletes teach you about what is most helpful to them.

In the end, it's up to you to try things out in practice. Your personal effectiveness and well-being was our motivation for writing this book. Good luck, as they say before you head out into action.

Acknowledgments

Many thanks to our editor, Jim Nageotte of The Guilford Press, who guided us through this book with such competence, and who made it fun too. Special thanks also to Mary Hodorowicz, who kept rereading drafts, never missing the details that matter. David Rosengren, Stefan Rollnick, and Jane Keislar read chapter drafts and obliged us to reconsider many things; thank you. Josh Lifrak, director of the Mental Skills Program for the Chicago Cubs baseball team, gave us his firsthand account of the story of their success in the World Series.

The initial spark for this book came from Imtiaz Ahmad, a medical doctor and much more, who works in elite soccer. When asked why he had come to a motivational interviewing workshop, he said, "I want to learn to listen better, change the culture of our club, and move away from the 'fit in or go away' approach to developing players." Then he helped coaches to learn motivational interviewing skills.

We thank James Vaughan for opening doors for us and for his creative work on the limitations of praise in his own development. Susan Klumpner from The Ace Project in the West Baltimore City tennis camp provided inspiration and vision about how to engage young people in sports. Similarly, Edu Rubio, an elite soccer coach, became a close friend who modeled good practice to all lucky enough to work with him. Richard Bailey in Berlin and Dominique Gobat from Lausanne gave freely to helpful conversations and stories about what works well in their settings.

From the world of cricket, we cannot thank enough Lynsey Williams and particularly Mark Wallace, who provided pointers on what a supportive sporting culture looks like, as did Ian Gough from the rugby world.

Psychologist Rory Mack has been alongside us from the start, with a keen eye on what motivational interviewing looks like and how coaches and athletes might benefit in everyday practice and competition. Our colleague Chris Wagner contributed much to our thinking about how people change, and we acknowledge his helpful comments about motivational interviewing and teamwork. Finally, when we ventured into the world of sports in poor communities, we were guided by the steady hand of baseball and softball coach Rob Maitra, so much so that he ended up giving his time to a chapter in this book.

Contents

PART I

MOTIVATIONAL INTERVIEWING

I was a high jumper on the U.S. squad for the 1972 Munich Olympics and one of the early adaptors of the technique called the "Fosbury flop." Unlike the traditional jump, you approached the bar and jumped over it backward and head first. After my athletic career ended, I changed direction, learned motivational interviewing (MI), and spent many years as a counselor in hospital settings helping people in and around trauma wards to consider how they could lead safer and healthier lives.

The flop and MI have a lot in common. They have both exploded in popularity and were inspired by an effort to take a different approach to a familiar problem, with the flop the challenge being to jump a bar backwards, and with MI to find a different way to assist people to change. Then there's a more direct link between them: MI can help someone to learn the flop.

I recently reunited with my old friend and fellow high jumper Dick Fosbury, the originator of the flop technique that bears his name. Nowadays, he runs a high-jump camp for teaching kids to flop. He told me that when he is coaching, after a kid takes a practice jump, they come over to him for advice, expecting to be told what's wrong and how they should try to correct the next jump. But instead, the first thing he asks them is, "What did you notice about the jump you just took?"

I can promise you that, unlike Dick, many coaches are quick to tell the kid that his curve was too wide, or his last step too long or slow. That kind of curious guiding question from Dick was how I refined my high-jump technique, and it could have come out of an MI practitioner's manual. It's what talented coaches and MI practitioners do—encourage the wisdom of the person to find their way. If you want an athlete to improve, easy as it might be to just tell them what to do, my experience tells me, "Watch it, hold back, let the athlete tell you," just as it was with those thousands of patients I met over the years. Learning how to do either the flop or MI takes practice, for sure, but it brings results.

—CHRIS DUNN, ex-Olympic high jumper and trainer in MI
(personal communication)

Here in this book is the roadmap, or that MI practitioner's manual, that Chris Dunn talks about above. A question like Dick Fosbury's can be a useful start to a conversation. What happens next can be even more powerful, which is where listening and summarizing come in. You probably use most skills anyway, perhaps without being aware of quite how they work and the impact they can have on motivation and performance. This first part of the book should help to clarify things for you.

Part I and the chapters to follow will give you a solid feel for the power of conversation to change lives and build excellence. We start by diving into sporting conversations and how MI can help to improve them (Chapter 1). Then we address, in turn, each of the following: your attitude and mindset (Chapter 2), the method and skills involved (Chapters 3 and 4), and, finally, two special topics, affirmation (Chapter 5) and resistance (Chapter 6)—both of which are designed to help you improve your ability to get the best out of the athletes you work with, even in difficult circumstances.

Part II looks at a range of MI strategies from connecting rapidly to improving motivation, setting goals, and giving advice skillfully. Part III turns to wider challenges, like how to use MI to build teamwork, to improve well-being and lifestyle, to support athletes from poor communities, and to improve the culture of a team.

Take note of Part IV, where we have placed some short summaries of key topics that you might like to keep handy as you learn the skills involved.

At the end of each chapter, we list some "Questions to Consider" that we might have raised were we on a training course with you, designed to stretch your thinking and improve your competence.

CHAPTER 1

A Different Approach

It's about the person. Technicals and tacticals follow that.
—NICK LEVETT, soccer coach

HIGHLIGHTS

+ Motivating athletes is a challenge at every level of sports.
+ Solving problems for athletes often backfires.
+ MI can be added to your coaching toolbox for helping athletes to lift motivation and realize their potential.

It's one thing to want someone to change and improve, but another to help them do it. In sports there are many moments when you try to help an athlete and then you wonder, *What's going to motivate them? What do I say now?* One simple answer, the foundation for motivational interviewing (MI), came from French philosopher Blaise Pascal, who captured it thus in the 17th century: "People are better persuaded by the reasons which they have themselves discovered than by those that come into the mind of others" (Pascal, 1670/1958). MI simply provides the tools for making this happen.

THE KICKOFF

Imagine a scenario where, whatever the pressure you are under, you and the athletes around you are in a great place, facing competition like champions, smart and effective. The setbacks might come rolling in and yet there you are, talking through the struggles and really supporting each other. You have many a tough conversation in and around this squad, and yet you

3

never sink into a destructive blame game. Problems get solved, relationships remain solid, and you laugh and move on, together. Over time, results improve.

Learning MI can help to open these doors, where conversation helps to improve relationships, motivation, and performance. The first part of this book provides a roadmap of what's involved, about how you can use improved relationships to have really effective conversations.

BETTER CONVERSATIONS, BETTER OUTCOMES?

"I want my athletes to be up there, free of doubt, trusting each other, feeling fit, focused, rested, and raring to go." In other words, you want them to be motivated—to enjoy their sport and master the skills that make a difference, not just as individuals but in teams too.

It's also a challenge faced outside of sports, helping people to be focused and committed to change, and MI emerged in the 1980s in a corner of the mental health field where this challenge could not be avoided.

FROM THE FRONTLINE

In my first job I was faced with a schedule full of people who needed motivating, in a center for treating addicts, surrounded by colleagues in the coffee room who were full of talk about which were the really motivated patients and what we needed to do with those who were not (the majority). The answer was more or less clear-cut: it was our job to motivate them, to eliminate all doubt about getting rid of drugs, to make them realize the folly of their ways, and to give them insight into why and how they should change. For their part, the patients were generally resistant to these efforts, and there was never any question that the fault lay with them and their lack of motivation. We sat back and blamed them, and our conversations were frustrating and combative—it never crossed my mind that there was an alternative to meeting force with force. It took a murder to wake me up. A quiet young man walked out of a group one day and shot his wife and then himself. MI was born a few years later when William R. Miller published a paper that turned the logic of motivating others upside down, and it went some distance to explaining what had been going wrong in that treatment center: there was another way of going about it. He and I became friends and collaborators, and some 35 years later MI has spread around many fields and been studied and supported by more than a thousand scientific studies. At its core, MI is about shining a light on what is good about people and using empathy to empower them to be part of the change process. Sports is an ideal home for MI because we all want to help athletes thrive, and that's the essential aim of MI too.

—S. R.

Let's take a look around the world of sports to meet some familiar athletes:

1. *The professional "diamond in the rough."* Age 19, riding high with his first big contract, and yet his diet seems all over the place. You raise the subject, and he says, "No, I'm fine thanks. I can look after myself these days."
2. *The low-morale team.* Your group of players is having a joyless time since losing important teammates in the off-season, and morale is low. Everything you try to change seems to be ignored.
3. *The total beginner.* You can see a problem in this runner's stride immediately after the starting gun, so you take a deep breath and say, "You did really well there, but can I just say that if you had only pushed a little harder right at the beginning of the race, you would have got into a groove earlier and done better. So that's something to think about for next time." The athlete looks distracted. No impact.

Now what? "If only they would listen to me," you probably grumble to yourself. You can see how making a change would help them, but can they? What can you do or say to them that might make a difference and help them move from saying things like, "No, thanks . . ." to "Maybe . . ." right up to "Yes, I really want to do that"?

All three scenarios above involve a coach who cared, who expressed the optimism and enthusiasm that sits at the heart of quality coaching. Yet caring was somehow not enough for lifting motivation and making progress.

WHAT DO YOU SAY NEXT?

Imagine that coach carrying on with the same strategy—solving the problem *for* athletes.

1. *The "diamond in the rough."* You might suggest, "Well, I'm sorry, but being at an elite level comes with responsibilities to look after your health and your diet. I'll get the nutritionist to have a word with you." His reply is, "Yes, *but* I know how to eat and how it affects me on the field. I mean, I don't go stuffing myself with junk food just before a game." You get pushback, and this diamond's motivation might have even gone down. He doesn't like to be told what to do. What happened to the trust you thought he had in you?
2. *The low-morale team.* You offer, "We all miss our colleagues, who made us so strong last season. I want us to really focus now and be positive, enjoy ourselves, and go for it this season, OK?" The team

captain thinks, *But what's the point?* The team looks at the ground, in dead silence. Your shot has missed its mark. Maybe there's something else preventing them from moving ahead. Do they trust you and each other?

3. *The total beginner.* With the runner you might continue, "Do you see what I mean? Start well and it will end well, if you get my meaning." He may reply, "Well, yes, *but* I was focusing on the middle part of the race, to be honest, because that's where I need to really focus and use all my best energy." A coach sees it one way, the athlete another. Any sign of the fire of motivation being lifted?

The strategy used here was to try harder to persuade them, to "make them see" the best way ahead and to "drive sense into" them.

Pushing Athletes Can Backfire

Did you notice the athletes' use of the word *but* in each of those three conversations above? Persuading, commanding, and solving problems *for* athletes are useful tools, and we will clarify why and how in the next chapter. However, if they are your *only* tools, and you use them routinely for every challenge, you could get tired and grumpy, and blame athletes for low motivation—and in turn they might respond with arguments, blank looks, sulking, or worse—feigning compliance ("Yes, thanks for the advice"). We use the term "righting reflex" to describe the reaction we have as coaches when see a problem and automatically assume, *without thinking,* that it's our job to "right it," to jump in and fix it. It's when there's a sudden rush to solve problems that mistakes are so often made. In the examples above, focusing on convincing athletes what they should do results in both parties falling into a persuasion trap. One sign we're approaching that trap is the word *but.* "Why don't you . . . ?" is met with, "Yes, *but* that won't work because . . . ," or another passive, even evasive, response. This kind of exchange becomes a trap because every time athletes use "but" to pivot away from the direction you want them to go, the fire of motivation inside them dies out a little bit more.

> "Yes, but . . ." from the athlete is a signal to change tack.

Here's what we discovered in MI: by using other tools from the toolbox, you can make it possible for athletes to stoke that fire for themselves. This is a practical way of realizing a widely held view in sports, revealed when football player and coach Homer Rice apparently said, "You can motivate by fear, and you can motivate by reward. But both those methods are only temporary. The only lasting thing is self-motivation."

MI: A DIFFERENT KIND OF CONVERSATION

What if our job is to motivate athletes *not* solely by advising, pushing, and persuading but through something else instead? Take a look at this conversation, and notice what happens. A coach wants to assist a runner to get going after an injury and feels she is probably a bit too hesitant for her own good.

COACH: How is that ankle feeling now?

ATHLETE: They say it's ready for the real thing. I'm not so sure.

COACH: How ready for action do you really feel?

ATHLETE: Yeah, well, I guess so, but what if I push it too far (*looking a bit doubtful*)?

COACH: You're not sure.

ATHLETE: Nah, but it might be OK; how can I tell?

COACH: You're wondering whether the ankle will take all the pressure.

ATHLETE: And yeah, I need to believe in myself too.

COACH: What's going to help you feel more confident?

ATHLETE: I want to try it out. I mean, I am determined to try it out under pressure, like maybe not full on but under pressure for, say, half an hour.

COACH: That feels like the right next step for you.

ATHLETE: It's got to be. I'm, like, ready for that, for sure.

The coach's attitude was one of helping the athlete find her own path to improvement. Instead of trying to instill ideas and motivation into her, he drew this out of her. That's MI. As with a technique to throw, catch, or run more efficiently, MI is way of doing things that can be powerful and effective.

If that exchange above reads like a normal-sounding conversation, it's no coincidence, because that's exactly what you want to aim for in using MI. It is simple, but as any athlete will tell you, learning a simple new play or adjustment is not necessarily easy. It initially takes a conscious effort to break free of old habits and work in a new way, and it takes practice to master. When it comes to MI, we must be willing to imagine that there are strengths and resources in that person that we cannot necessarily put our finger on but believe are there. Notice the use of the word *person*—it will only be a normal conversation if you see them as people first, athletes second.

Now consider one of the skills used by that coach, what we call a listening statement. It's a technical device for expressing empathy, a foundation of MI.

Empathy Used as a Motivator

You might have heard about the power of empathy. As we will show you, it is possible to channel empathy in ways that motivate athletes to do better. It happened in that conversation with the runner above.

Empathy means "standing in another's shoes" or imagining their experience, not the same as sympathy or feeling sorry for someone. Athletes feel and appreciate it, and it can and has become an essential ingredient in successful coaching that improves connection and helps athletes to make progress. In MI empathy is used not only to build a relationship but also to promote behavior change. This is achieved with a technical skill, something you say to the athlete, what we call a listening statement. Looking back at that conversation above, this technique was used three times. You can spot its use by the absence of a question mark and the presence of a statement, not a question.

> In MI, empathy is used to promote behavior change.

Here's how it works. You start by trying to imagine what it must be like for the athlete, "to stand in his or her shoes." Then a critical second step: you convey this to the athlete in the form of a statement, as that coach does above, for example, by saying, "You're wondering whether the ankle will take all the pressure." The athlete will sense your empathy, curiosity, and desire to understand; take the conversation baton from you; and run with it. She replies to that statement with "And yeah, I need to believe in myself too." Right there she is expressing *greater commitment to taking the next step,* and her motivation is improving as she says it. That's the simple art of MI: She is talking herself into changing, rather than relying on the coach to do this for her. What researchers have uncovered by analyzing conversation is that the more people say things like this, the more likely they are to act on their own advice.

Doubt Is Normal

This next aspect of MI might come as a surprise: Doubt and low motivation are viewed not as problems but as keys to unlocking progress. It's a question of how you handle a conflict that we call "ambivalence," a topic to be covered in many places in this book (see Chapter 3).

Athletes seem to thrive on overcoming that battle between optimism and doubt, and yet sometimes we see doubt winning over, to affect their focus, confidence, and performance. We saw this above in those three examples that opened the chapter: "Should I do something about my diet?" (the diamond in the rough); "Maybe our team will work together more now or maybe not" (the low-morale team); or "I might focus on the early part of the race, but I'm not sure" (the total beginner).

People seesaw between "staying just as I am" and "making the change that might be worthwhile." Were those athletes in the examples above really *only* thinking of one side of their doubt, the negative side? Unlikely. The rough diamond, despite his denial about his diet, was probably at least a bit concerned about it. The depleted team might be feeling down, but they have turned up, also wanting to do better. And the race runner might have also wondered about pushing harder at the beginning of the race. Doubt reigned supreme. It's when they are in this state of doubt that using a direct approach so often backfires.

> A direct approach backfires when an athlete feels doubtful.

Let Them Make the Case for Change

Imagine how a conversation might go if instead of you making the case for change, the athlete does. Recall the persuasion trap we discussed above (the "righting reflex"). If you spell out all the reasons a change is a good idea, it's as if athletes flick a switch in their minds and start telling you why the change is *not* a good idea. As they hear themselves say this, they become even more convinced *not* to change. Their motivation starts heading down, not up. Athletes are not alone in this. Most people like to make up their minds for themselves. MI involves helping them to unscramble their doubt and give voice to what will lift their motivation, not lower it.

How might you do this, let's say with those three athletes above? Our best advice is to step aside for a moment, take a short breather, and then find a way of letting them make the case for change, a bit like lifting your head up in a game and looking for a pass. A question is a good move to start with, like an invitation to face change; you feed them the ball with a question and then let them take it and move forward.

- *Scenario 1:* To the "rough diamond," the coach might have asked, "How might you do a little better with your diet?"
- *Scenario 2:* The team that is depleted and feeling down might have been asked, "How can we take the first step to improving this

season? What would that look like for you? What would you enjoy doing more of in practice?"
- *Scenario 3:* The racing athlete might have been asked, "How might you make better progress at the beginning of the race?"

You'll notice that the questions all have a searching, forward-looking quality, designed to get the athletes to sift through the answers. You switch from a stance captured by "I have all the answers" to one captured with "What do you think? Let's look at this together." The player will more than likely start talking about change, about some of the difficulties, but also about how and why it could come about. Their positive statements about change are what we call *"change talk."* You get the player thinking about the benefits of making the change, and the means to making it happen.

What About Your Expertise?

You might well be thinking at this point, *Hang on a minute. My job is to notice what's needed and make sure I get my message across. And this athlete hardly knows what she needs. How can I hand the baton over to her?* Think of it like this: the more you invest in uncovering the athletes' point of view, the more interested they will be in yours. Then when the time comes to take back control and offer advice, it's more likely to be heard and acted on. If you dance rather than wrestle in a conversation with athletes, learning happens in front of your eyes.

FROM THE FRONTLINE

There's a saying that coaches use in some teams that goes like this: "You don't have to be sick to get better." Its use highlights an attitude to athlete improvement that has roots in the psychologist Carol Dweck's research on why some people give up too easily but others make noticeable improvement (Dweck, 2017). Her advice to sports coaches is to help athletes develop a "growth mindset," to see setbacks as learning opportunities. If they adopt a fixed mindset—for example, "My inborn talent is all I need to progress"—they risk failing to reach their potential because their mistakes are seen as problems, something wrong with them, to be avoided or to feel bad about. Athletes in this state of mind tend not to stretch themselves and give up too easily. To get better and improve, so the logic goes, a growth mindset has athletes willing to take on harder tasks because they will see mistakes as opportunities to stretch and enjoy themselves. They focus on the learning, not just the outcome.

MI is a practical way of encouraging this growth mindset. Pointing out faults and using the righting reflex at every turn will not lift motivation and performance as much as supporting athletes to take risks, free of fear of judgment, and to get into the flow and focus on the process of their athletic effort. This book is geared toward realizing this approach through conversation.

The Benefits

MI is just one way to help athletes improve, and it's not the only road for all coaches and athletes. "Try it and see" would be our advice, not just once but a few times, and even ask the athletes how helpful your conversation was and what might improve it.

You might be wondering about what evidence there is for the effectiveness of MI. While there's lots of literature on using MI in many fields—and it points squarely at the power of listening and valuing the resourcefulness of the person you are speaking to—MI is new to sports. However, there is probably more immediate evidence right in front of you: If you hear and see the athlete talking brightly about the possibility of change, this tells you that you are getting something right. Keep going. If you hear the opposite, it's a signal to change course. Just as we know the likely progress of a game, even outside a stadium, by the noise of the fan reactions, we can assess the effectiveness of our coaching conversation by closely watching our players' reactions to what we say. In this way your athletes are giving you real-time feedback, and they effectively become your teacher.

Here are some of the benefits we've observed in our work with coaches:

Improved Relationships

As coaches, we all highlight the importance of having good relationships with teammates. The more you put into building relationships, the better the outcomes will be. That said, it can be difficult to know just *how* to improve relationships with individual athletes and the team as whole. MI calls for setting up a foundation of trust and mutual respect, and *there are skills you can practice daily to achieve this* (Chapter 4).

Improved Performance and Well-Being

Every team is looking for the next edge. If you kindle the fire of motivation inside athletes, their performance should improve. This will in turn improve well-being. MI is about the athlete *doing things* differently. In other fields, such as health care, MI has been credited for improving behavior on a wide range of fronts.

In Brief Exchanges

In sports we are often pressed for time. MI can be used in very brief conversations, in and around the field of play, to encourage creative decision making and bind the threads of linked conversations over time. Indeed, the more skillful you are, the less time it will take to have effective conversations.

When There's Conflict—with Individuals and in Teams

As coaches, we are often also referees. MI emerged from settings rich in conflict, and it is designed to alleviate, minimize, and even eliminate it. We have noticed that the skills of MI can be used not just to resolve doubt and lift motivation but also in numerous tight corners where trouble is brewing, in difficult relationships with athletes, with problem behaviors, or when a group or squad is sliding backward.

In a Culture That Champions the Love of Sports

Most coaches are trying to build a strong, positive culture for their team. Sport is full of slogans and mission statements that talk about improving culture, enjoyment, and good relationships, yet these good intentions are all too often driven sideways by obsession with profit, results at all cost, and the shabby treatment of those who don't succeed. Our clear bias is toward getting the process right; building better relationships using the practical skills described in this book will produce better outcomes of all kinds, including in results themselves. When we help athletes to express themselves, say what they think and feel, and talk about change, our relationships improve and we change the culture there and then, bit by bit. We notice that coaches who are remembered with the most respect are those who treated players as people, not just as athletes, and kept a keen eye on their sense of self-worth and journey through life, and who took concrete steps to support players off the field. MI provides a roadmap for doing this.

Of Benefit to You?

Your desire to support athletes most likely motivated you to pick up this book. No one can say it's easy being a coach, having to keep an eye on so many things, or that you won't make mistakes. Your well-being also deserves to take center stage so you can help players reach for their dreams. Preserving your energy, not wasting it in needless argument, and channeling your conversations into efficient efforts to build motivation and performance are some of the benefits of improving your communication skills. The more you feel you can "be yourself," comfortable in your own skin, genuinely expressing optimism in the potential of athletes, the easier it will be to use MI and to enjoy the conversations. The work of improving your communication in this simple but powerful way gives you a new outlet to improve and measure your success. It's not just about results. Instead of only reflecting on your win/loss record, a new path emerges, one that has you as a leader who will be the best you can be no matter what the record is.

THIS BOOK

You can approach this book in many ways. The list of chapter titles should help you to locate the topics of greatest relevance. You might wonder, for example, what we mean by "resistance" in difficult situations, in which case reading Chapter 6 will give you a feel for how MI might be helpful, or you might be interested in teamwork. Chapters 11 and 12 look at practical things you can do with MI to build morale and togetherness, even in those challenging team meetings or halftime talks.

Whichever route you take, you'll notice the book overall offers you a shift in mindset, which is why you might do best to read Chapter 2 before jumping to later chapters. There, you'll get a good feel for how MI can be viewed as an extension of a familiar coaching style in which you guide rather than command. That's the platform for MI, and principles and skills are described after that, in Chapters 3 and 4.

YOUR CHOICE

When your usual approaches are not working, where do you go next? We all know that nagging feeling that something wasn't quite right in a conversation with an athlete. We also know what if feels like to really nail it. Our experience working alongside some of the world's most successful coaches suggests that flexibility is key. They think about what's going to make a difference, and they shift their approach, because what works with some athletes falls flat with others.

There's clearly no single way to lift motivation, which is why building up a coaching toolbox is in order. The famous psychologist Abraham Maslow is reported to have said, "If you only have a hammer, you tend to see every problem as a nail." You don't just want a hammer in your hand for banging away at every challenge. You inspire players, encourage them gently, use tough love, make jokes, and sometimes say nothing, simply observing and letting them learn from their own mistakes. MI can be there in the toolbox so you can take advantage of those many opportunities to motivate athletes that arise in corridors, in locker rooms, and on the field itself.

QUESTIONS TO CONSIDER

- What drew you into working in sports?
- What's the most significant conversation you have had in your sporting life? Why was it so important?
- Are you different with athletes depending on whether you like them?
- If good relationships in sports are important, then why is so little attention paid to this in education and training?

CHAPTER 2

Mindset

You can motivate players better with kind words
than you can with a whip.
                    —BUD WILKINSON, athlete and coach

HIGHLIGHTS

+ Get sharper at switching your mindset across three coaching styles: fixing, guiding, and following. Guiding is the foundation for MI.
+ Tame the righting reflex: (1) warm up, (2) take deep breaths, and (3) recover if you lapse.
+ Skillful guiding: (1) connect first, (2) inquire about a way forward, (3) offer advice with choices, (4) develop joint action plans, and (5) remember the conversation for next time.

THE KICKOFF

Whatever your role in sports, when things get busy you can sometimes get so bogged down in detail that you lose sight of the bigger picture. Finding that balance is a bit like trying to be an eagle (the overview) and a mouse (the detail) at the same time. It's a zone that athletes on the field know well. If you get too lost in the detail, you can be in trouble.

How would you handle this situation?

FROM THE FRONTLINE

Two young athletes are fighting, with voices raised and faces hot with anger. One of them playfully tripped the other who lost his temper, and now they are facing each other, heads a few inches apart. Now what? While your main focus will be on preventing injury and getting on with the job, is there also some way you turn this into a learning opportunity for them? You walk up to them and say what exactly, and why?

Your mindset is going to be important in this conversation. You will want to be clear about the horizon, the approach you will take (the eagle), and also quite skilled in handling the conversation content, the moment-to-moment accusations that are highly likely to come your way (the mouse). You will want to be both "inside" and "outside" of the conversation at the same time. Not always so easy.

You might well choose to use a fixing style ("I plan to solve this problem for them"): You take them aside and make it clear they need to find better ways of handling things that are less disruptive for all concerned. Your mindset, the words you use, and your body language will be all important. You try to make sure you are responding, not just reacting. That's a good example of a fixing style working reasonably well. As long as you are calm and trustworthy, you may be able to take the heat out of the situation. You have probably solved the immediate problem, but a question still remains: What have they really learned about how to control their emotions a bit better? Was your horizon a bit narrow? Where was the eagle heading?

Other approaches to a standoff like that are possible, and our best advice is to think of a fixing style a bit like you might add spices in a dish of food: best used with restraint, aware of what dish you are trying to make and the value of other ingredients that help athletes to learn. Before turning to what we call a guiding style, where you help athletes to learn new ways of handling challenges, we will address the pitfalls of a fixing style, because recognizing the warning signs will enable you step back and consider other horizons you might aim for.

THE DOWNSIDE OF FIXING

We described in Chapter 1 how trying to persuade someone to change often results in resistance and pushback. It's not fixing as such that's the problem, but overusing it as your only style for coaching, what we called using the righting reflex. Athletes tend to switch off too often. Fixing becomes not the spice in a dish but the only ingredient you use, and your job becomes that of the *deficit detective* searching this way and that for things that are wrong, when you might do better to work with athletes' strengths. Put simply, when we fix less, it works more. Consider this familiar coaching moment:

FROM THE FRONTLINE

It's a big game. As the coach, you are feeling the weight of it all. The pressure to lead, and to fulfill expectations, is strong. You want to create an environment that allows for a positive team dynamic. You feel responsible to guide those players who are lost and ensure others who are playing well continue to do so.

You enter the locker room feeling focused as you remind your players of their job and the team's goals (a fixing style). Sensing a good energy in the room, you join the team as the group runs out onto the field. The game begins.

Almost immediately, that confident feeling disappears as the team seems to forget everything you ever told them. The captain even appears to be leading the group in a way that is almost exactly contrary to your coaching methods. They end up losing badly.

After the game, a key moment comes. You approach the captain to clarify what went wrong. You're firm and clear and talk about how things might be improved next time. He is quiet, even when you ask him if he has any questions or thoughts. As you leave the facility, you see him sitting in front of his locker looking deflated. You feel as though you might have missed something—an opportunity to connect, or to teach—but you don't see a path to getting through to him.

Could this happen to you? Is a fixing style the only approach you might use?

When things go wrong and emotion is running high, it's harder to restrain the righting reflex, and that's when a fixing style can be least effective. You probably know the experience: your head hurts from seeing athletes getting it wrong, and you step in and put it right for them. As coaches, it's understandable that we fall into this mindset and want to jump in and fix things. The demand to fix is everywhere—from parents, other coaches, administration, fans, and even the players themselves. For this reason, the overuse of fixing is so widespread in sports that it warrants waving a red flag in coaching education, in locker rooms, and on the side of the field.

> When we fix less, it works more.

FROM THE FRONTLINE

What's the best way to help someone who sits on the precipice of a bridge threatening to jump off and commit suicide? How about helping hostage takers change their minds? When working with first responders and hostage negotiators, it became clear to me that using the righting reflex by trying to grab people and forcing them down was probably the least effective approach. These brave and highly trained individuals talk about a quite different mindset. They will tell you that the best approach is to engage people "where they are at," to form a relationship, and to discuss *their* view of their problems. You keep this up until individuals can calm down and it makes sense to either tactically pull them off the ledge or coax them off the ledge of their own free will.

—J. F.

The link to athlete motivation is this: an athlete may seem to be in an unproductive place—unmotivated, conflicted, angry, or seemingly unable to take our directions or coaching advice. But when we view them as they are, on a ledge so to speak, unsure if they should come down and talk to us or jump, we can be more effective in helping them by taking the approach used by these highly trained first responders. We can approach them and focus on their view of the situation. Thus we create a connection that allows them to see our perspective and perhaps contemplate changing their behavior or their approach to the sport.

In challenging situations with athletes, we too are probably in a state of physiological arousal (stressed, frustrated, and concerned). Our heart may be racing, or we may be feeling tense. We are more likely to be tempted to fix the problem, quickly and directly. Yet this is precisely the time when the techniques and style of MI might be most needed. Step 1 for first responders is to be calm.

Taming the Righting Reflex

It is hard to listen before you have "tamed" the righting reflex. In order to do that we recommend these practical steps:

1. *Have a warm-up for yourself.* Before a conversation that you know will be tense, have a warm-up in which you remind yourself of the purpose of the conversation—for example: "I want to start by simply listening to this player during the next few minutes." It may be helpful also to explain your intentions to the player—for example: "Jimmy, I would just like to take a few minutes to understand your perspective." This commitment to yourself and to the player may help a great deal in staying focused and resisting the righting reflex.

2. *Take a few deep breaths.* There's a wide body of research that suggests that regulating your heart rate by breathing slowly can help keep you calm in sports and other settings. Take a couple of deep breaths before you have an important conversation to help slow you down.

3. *A lapse is not a relapse.* During your conversation, you may get frustrated and tense, but remind yourself periodically, "It's never too late to turn it around." At any point in the conversation, you can always apologize to athletes and remind him- or herself (and your-self) of your hopes for finding what might be really helpful to him or her—for example: "Hold on a second, Maria. Let me back up. I'm

Aim for a calm heart and an uncluttered mind.

sorry—I got a little carried away there. It's just that I'm really passionate about helping you be at your best. Please tell me your point of view on this."

It's one thing to want to help; it's another to get into a mindset that will serve you and your athletes best. You want your heart to be involved, but not racing along, and you want your mind to be free of this or that idea, plan, or piece of feedback.

YOUR CHOICE OF STYLES

When we ask coaches about their mindset, they often say things like "You either tell them what to do [fix], or leave them free to make up their own minds [follow]":

"I'm a bit 'old school,' a tough taskmaster, while some of my other coach friends are a bunch of pushovers and loose about it all."
"Too many players are overcoached. I prefer to let them be free and creative."
"I'm an expert with skills to teach them. Their job is to listen and practice hard."
"Sometimes I tell them what to do; other times I leave them free to do it for themselves."
"I'm a 'player's coach.'"

Our journeys through education, sports, parenting, and health care suggests there is a third style that sits midway between those two choices, either to fix or to follow, and we call this a guiding style. It's a mindset that can be seen in the work of really talented coaches and teachers in which you encourage athletes by coming alongside and using your expertise to bring the best out of them, championing and affirming their mastery and enjoyment of new learning as it unfolds (see Figure 2.1).

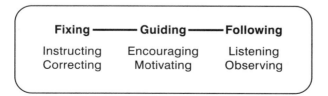

FIGURE 2.1. Three coaching styles.

Fixing

When fixing, you take the lead and tell an athlete why, what, or how they should perform. It's useful for solving simple and obvious problems, when asked for advice, or when you are organizing activities for individuals or a group. In this mindset you are less likely to try to understand the athlete's thoughts or perspectives about the situation or change; this is all about you getting *your* point across.

Following

Following is called for when it's time for you to observe, or if in conversation, to listen and allow the athlete to take the lead, such as when they are upset, angry, or wanting to get a message across to you. Listening can be helpful to athletes beyond our imaginations. It can also be the biggest challenge for coaches, because while you are listening, truly listening, for a short time you are not in control.

Guiding

Guiding is best for learning new skills and for solving more complex problems. It involves trust and working together, and talking about change and improvement, each taking a leading role. You point the conversation in the right direction and create an opportunity for athletes to motivate themselves and provide the solutions. You will also step forward and offer advice here and there, and then help athletes to choose the ideas that make the most sense. This style is the foundation for MI because the energy, bright ideas, and motivation for change come from the player, well captured by a colleague who said, "I guide, you decide."[1]

How then do you know which style to use and when? We couldn't put this more clearly than the way a baseball coach responded to the model presented above in Figure 2.1: "I get it. If I stand like this with my two feet planted firmly in the middle ground, in the guiding style, I can use that as my main approach to working with athletes, knowing that if I need to I can move either side toward fixing or following." This coach is pointing out that it's not which approach you should use, it's when you should use which approach! Most coaches need to fix sometimes, but when they do so after following and guiding, the fixing is more powerful and long lasting.

---

[1] With thanks to Rick Reyes.

GUIDING: TWO EXPERTS AND A STRONG RELATIONSHIP

The idea of working together captures two essential features of guiding: the relationship is central, and both parties have important perspectives to offer. This is more than being friendly on your part. Often it has nothing at all to do with being friendly. It does not rely solely on the chemistry between you. It takes effort and skill, and it involves connecting with athletes in the present, leaving them feeling understood and supported.

We have identified four key elements to the mindset of a sporting guide, each of which can be spotted in the way you conduct your conversations.

Reach Out and Connect

This first element of skillful guiding can be spotted as a golden rule in every coach's handbook: "Form an effective relationship." Yet there are different ways of reaching out to and connecting with athletes. Consider this typical example:

Coaching as Usual

"I know you're new here, so I wanted to reach out and go over some of the ground rules about how we do things. Let me know if you have any questions as I go along."

That seems fair enough as an introduction, and yet how good is the connection from a coach who is also conveying the message "I am in charge" so strongly? Is it just a routine line trotted out as a greeting, or does this coach really care about the athlete? Is there a way of connecting a little more deeply to begin with?

The mindset shift when using MI might be expressed like this:

Coaching with Guiding

"I know you're new here and you probably have some questions about how the place operates. I'd like to start with getting to know more about you. Tell me about what you would most like to get out of being with us here?"

This more personal reaching out is going to help quite considerably with building a relationship. Skillful guides want to know about the person they are working with, and from the athlete's perspective, first impressions matter. If you think of it like an investment, the more you put in, the more you can reap rewards further down the line. If we try to spend too much before we build up capital, we go into debt. Stay in debt for too long, and the relationship will default. Skills for connecting rapidly with athletes are discussed and illustrated in detail in Chapter 8.

A Person, Not Just an Athlete

Then there's a second element to guiding: treating athletes as people first, athletes second. What do you make of this everyday call from a coach to an athlete to concentrate better?

Coaching as Usual

"Patrick, I don't know what's going on with you, but your mind just isn't here and it needs to be. So, whatever it is, get it figured out."

This coach is being direct and clear, but how limited is this intervention by only seeing the athlete, not the person, when it's quite likely that something personal could be distracting the athlete in the first place? A coach using a guiding style might speak very differently:

Coaching with Guiding

"Pat, it seems like something is on your mind. What's going to help you feel more settled?"

The effect of talking with a person, not just an athlete, is that you are showing respect for and interest in what the person is thinking and feeling. The benefit of this is that deeper knowledge and connection may lead to greater success in communicating about the person's performance as an athlete or role in a team.

Opportunities to communicate in a guiding style arise in countless situations, and as long as you are genuine, you can be sure athletes will appreciate this. One of the grand illusions surrounding sports is that athletes are, or should be, automatons, soldiers, or robots with a limited range of emotions, aggression, and competitiveness being the most commonly reinforced. Skillful coaches will embrace a much wider range of emotions and reactions in the athletes they work with. Indeed, recollections from successful athletes are littered with examples of the value of caring and support from those around them. The most successful coaches seem to have one thing in common: they care about the *people* they work with. Ignore this human element and MI can't even get off the ground.

Someone with Strengths

Guiding athletes requires that you recognize and make use of a third frequently ignored element: their strengths. Imagine there are two pairs of glasses you could wear, one that sees mainly weakness or deficits, the other strengths. Wearing the strengths lenses does not mean you ignore weaknesses or problems but rather that you notice and use the athletes' strengths to address them (see Chapter 5 on how to use affirmation in addition to praise). Consider these two contrasting statements about the same athlete:

Coach A

"I can't believe how she plays. She always seemed to be in her own bubble, not aware of others around her. That's why she never passes. She doesn't look up much at all. We need to get that right. I'll talk to her."

This coach is taking on the role of a *deficit detective,* looking through deficit lenses and seeing an athlete first, a person second.

Coach B

"She's got power for sure, and she lunges forward with really good effect. Her head's often down, and I wonder, what is her awareness of the other players coming up alongside? Maybe her confidence is a bit low today? I'll link up with her and see how she thinks she can improve; then, if there's a good opening in our conversation, I'll share some of my thoughts too."

This coach notices problems but is also wearing strengths lenses and sees the person as well as the athlete.

Freedom of Choice

Then there's another element of guiding: respect for choice.

Coaching as Usual

"Listen, Chris. If you want to get better, then you must practice keeping your head up and your eyes downfield. If you don't, then I'm going to have to look at making a change."

We think of this as autonomy or a sense of independence, and there are few truisms in behavioral science that hold more weight than the observation that people like to feel free to make up their own mind about making changes in their lives. In coaching, a guide gives advice by providing choices, allowing people to explore, consider, and select one that makes sense to them. As athletes express why and how they might change, their motivation is lifted, which is where MI is central. In an MI mindset, we work toward providing as much choice as possible. That's the subject of Chapter 10, where providing information and advice can be transformed into an art form. The outcome is an athlete who wants to learn more.

Coaching with Guiding

"Chris, I've noticed something about you on the field. Do you have a minute? [Waits for Chris to nod.] I notice your head starts to drop when the ball comes near. I am wondering what you've observed?"

FROM THE FRONTLINE

There's a model of behavior change that's widely used in education and sports that fits very well with MI and using the style of a guide. It comes from self-determination theory (Ryan & Deci, 2000), and one of the key guidelines is this: People learn best if you meet their basic human needs for autonomy (freedom to choose), relatedness (supportive relationships), and competence (to develop and master new skills). Many of the skills and strategies of MI are designed to meet these needs and allow *internal* motivation to drive their progress.

GUIDING: IN PRACTICE

Moving from principles to practice, here are some key pointers to getting it right:

• *Connect with the athlete*. Make the best use of a following style to begin with. Listen and empathize with athletes' experience. The more skillful we are at listening well, the less time it will take: A few well-timed words are often worth more than many mouthfuls of advice or a long lecture. See Chapter 4 on the skills involved and Chapter 7, which is devoted to the task of rapid connecting.

• *Inquire about the best way forward*. Curiosity is the starting point. The most powerful questions are the ones we don't know the answer to about the athletes' experience. What is the athlete's perspective on the thing to be improved? Trust the judgment of the athlete to locate the

Curiosity is a good starting point.

problem and, indeed, to express the seeds of a solution. As coaches, we may be experts on a particular sport, but the MI view is that all athletes are the expert on themselves and how and why they might change. An athletes' motivation will improve as they hear themselves talk about change. Chapter 3 gets into this in depth.

• *Offer expert advice with choices.* Asking permission helps ("Would you be interested in learning a bit about what I have found to help other players in your position?"). Provide advice in the form of choices wherever possible; this helps athletes to make choices that suit them best while being more open to your perspective as an expert. See Chapter 10 on skillful advice.

• *Develop action plans.* Ask questions about the athletes' readiness and how much interest in and commitment to the plan they have. Jointly produce a flexible plan that is open to adjustment as progress unfolds. See Chapter 9.

• *Stay present, be patient, and pay attention. Remember the conversation so you can refer back to them when the timing is right.* The relationship gets stronger as two experts build on conversations over time.

TRAIN YOURSELF TO OBSERVE

The ability to step back and observe can be practiced and worked on, and it can be noticed in the work of successful coaches, teachers, and all practitioners who strive to support athletes. A skillful guide will be watching carefully to make sure that he or she provides the most useful route to success. Applied to the world of conversation, a skillful MI practitioner will focus on observing what's happening in the relationship and the conversation.

FROM THE FRONTLINE

Alex Ferguson is one of the most successful managers and coaches. His sport was soccer. In 2012 the Harvard Business School conducted a study of his methods. From one of the many interviews with him came this reflection about a key milestone in his development (Elberse, 2013):

> Once I stepped out of the bubble, I became more aware of a range of details, and my performance level jumped. Seeing a change in a player's habits or a sudden dip in his enthusiasm allowed me to go further with him: Is it family problems? Is he struggling financially? Is he tired? What kind of mood is he in? Sometimes I could even tell that a player was injured when he thought he was fine.

> I don't think many people fully understand the value of observing. I came to see observation as a critical part of my management skills. The ability to see things is key—or, more specifically, the ability to see things you don't expect to see.

Being open to the unexpected in conversation and observing how the athlete is responding, while at the same time being present and authentic within it, is a skill that can be worked on.

KEEP THE FIRE BURNING

Imagine yourself camping on a cold night. The sun has almost set, and you are frantically trying to get a fire going using less than dry wood. Frustrated, tired, and cold, you need that energy, big time. Athletes' motivation and desire to learn is like a fire inside them. Tap into this desire with the right mindset to ensure you don't snuff out this fire with unskillful coaching messages. Athletes' spirit and drive can be tapped into by seeing them as people with strengths and wisdom about the best way forward. If you hold off sharing your wisdom initially, and focus instead on enquiring about their perspective, your relationship will be strengthened and you'll be able to use practical skills to breathe life into their fire. It will then be easier to find the right moment to share your expertise and ensure it has maximum impact. If while camping you had calmly given the fire just the right amount of flint, air, and kindling it needed, it would quickly turn into a blaze that warmed up your night. The next chapter describes what motivation is and where MI can be used to harness it.

QUESTIONS TO CONSIDER

- When you were learning to drive, you probably occasionally got flustered as you tried to attend to many things at the same time. Eventually the new routines became familiar and easier to handle. It could be the same when adjusting your communication with athletes. What's the best way for you to start making progress on this front?
- Why do some athletes like to be told what to do, while others want to work things out for themselves?
- How does guiding fit into how you routinely work?

CHAPTER 3

Method

A lot of people notice when you succeed,
but they don't see what it takes to get there.
—DAWN STALEY, basketball coach

HIGHLIGHTS

+ Efforts to motivate "from the outside" can backfire.

+ Athletes can motivate themselves when guided to do so with empathy and the tools of MI.

+ MI at its core involves noticing "change talk" and searching for more.

"What's it going to take for you to play your best?" An athlete once came back a week later and said that this question had a powerful effect on her. It was the mindset of a guide that prompted it, a belief that she had the answer inside her. Now she wanted to talk it through and the next step was simply not to get in the way of her answering it, which is where MI came in.

THE KICKOFF

It might sound a bit crazy to use a phrase like "way of being" to describe using MI, but consider for a moment what that first responder described in Chapter 2, wanting to coax someone off a bridge. "A way of being" is exactly the phrase they will use to describe their mindset. MI starts with a different approach to motivation and to the language of motivation, and it feels quite different. It is not something you do *to* or *on* someone but a conversation you have *with* someone, on that person's behalf. It is through the

MI is not something you do to someone but a conversation you have with someone.

development of a strong relationship, a deep curiosity about the athlete as a person, and skillful guiding, that motivation is uncovered and enhanced. That deep curiosity is what psychologists often call empathy, an ability to stand in another's shoes.

FROM THE FRONTLINE

There are few teams in soccer more accomplished than the Liverpool Football Club. Looking back, a former coach Michael Beale said this: "Over the course of my time at Liverpool, I realized something. I'd got there as a good coach—but, really, it had very little to do with coaching. It had more to do with how I managed people. Whether they would take the message from me. How motivated I could get them" (Beale, 2018).

MOTIVATION

Where Does Motivation Come From?

If we are going to be effective in harnessing and helping our athletes develop motivation, it is important to first understand what this looks like and where it might come from. There are different sources for motivation; they vary across athletes and often change over time as athletes' career phase changes. To begin with, it's often internally driven (fun, challenge, mastery) while later it can be external (life after sports, financial security; Wylleman & Lavallee, 2004). Some get motivation from the inspiration they feel when they see others striving and succeeding against great odds. Some are motivated by the adversity they experience, some by their families, and some by their ambition—a burning desire to be the best. What motivates one athlete will fail utterly with another. It turns out that where motivation comes from is intensely personal and unique for each one of us.

What Lifts Motivation?

Now, let's imagine a list of the most common things coaches do to lift motivation. Mostly, when we think of increasing motivation we think of a list of tools or coaching tactics to address these players. That list will likely have methods that refer to inspiration. This usually means providing examples or encouragement that convinces athletes that they must dig deeper and make a greater effort.

Another approach to lifting motivation on this list is the tough love approach. This happens when we refuse to offer pity or sympathy to an athlete who is weary or discouraged. An example of this would be the coach who says, "You better toughen up, Buttercup, because it is going to get a lot worse before it gets better." This kind of approach sometimes jars athletes into realizing they are giving in too soon and must pace themselves for their journey.

Another kind of motivation might be encouraging or sympathizing. Coaches using this approach might say something like "I can see it hurts, but do you have one more sprint in you? Just one more, then we can stop. Just one." Another example of building motivation comes when coaches back off expectations and advise rest. "Your motivation is flagging—it's time for a day off. We don't want to overtrain." One final example of an approach to enhancing motivation is to use humor. One legendary pitching coach would regularly approach a struggling pitcher on the mound with jokes that would have to be censored on daytime television! Coaches using this approach often tell funny stories or jokes to engage and prepare their athletes. What other ways do you have on your list that we didn't think of?

What Approach Works Best?

Here is the interesting thing about all these different ways of lifting motivation: they all work sometimes, *and* they all have a cost. Let's think of a cost that might come with each of those approaches mentioned above:

- *Inspiration:* Athletes can feel they are never as good as the inspiring story or person being shown. Moreover, inspiration can fade because it's not personal to the particular athlete.
- *Tough love:* Athletes can feel defensive or resentful.
- *Encouraging or sympathizing:* This can make athletes dependent on approval for their motivation.
- *Humor:* This can backfire into criticism or mockery. Athletes might feel their doubts or reservations are being dismissed.
- *Resting/avoiding:* This can result in learning to give up when more effort is actually needed.

MOTIVATIONAL INTERVIEWING

It is easy to see why lifting motivation is such a complex topic—there are so many ways for you to win and lose at the same time. For just a minute, let's see how MI might work to lift motivation a bit differently.

How Is This Different from What You're Doing Now?

You start with the curious mindset of a guide described in Chapter 2. Then consider these key features of MI:

- MI is a conversation. It is about people talking to each other, usually face-to-face, often just the two of them, and sometimes in a group.
- MI is a forward-looking conversation about change of any kind, often in behavior.
- In MI, unlike the other methods above, the coach assumes the athletes already have within them all the motivation they need to be successful, but something is blocking it. That something is usually that the athletes are unsure about what they are doing. Why? It could be for an almost infinite number of reasons, including toxic thoughts, fear of success, off-the-field issues, not remembering their goals for training and competing, and fearing failure.
- The answer, in MI, is not to confront these reasons directly but to encourage athletes to find a way around them. We do this using the athlete's own language.
- Instead of telling athletes what to do or think, we draw that out of them (remember: it's in there; we don't have to supply it). How do we draw it out?

Have a look at the example below between a coach and an athlete, Kristin:

COACH: I've noticed you've been having some challenges lately with your sprint times.

KRISTIN: Everyone goes through a low spot, I guess.

COACH: It feels temporary to you.

KRISTIN: Yeah, I hope so.

COACH: You want to work at it.

KRISTIN: I do want to break my 60-meter time, but that probably means adding morning workouts. I don't know if I can stand two-a-days.

COACH: You're not sure it's worth it. But a part of you is really focused on that 60-meter time.

KRISTIN: Exactly.

COACH: What is it about that 60 meter that drives you forward like this?

KRISTIN: Because it is never going to be easier for me to be faster than right now. I'm in peak condition, and I can physically tolerate the two-a-days. I don't have a job after school like the other kids, so I can devote myself to conditioning. If I'm ever going to do it, it should be now. Later, that window might close, but now it's open if I go for it.

COACH: It's like an opening to take a shot.

KRISTIN: Yes.

COACH: Well, what's next?

KRISTIN: Really, all I have to do is get my backside out of bed earlier. Morning workouts aren't really so bad, and they're not forever. I can stand it until the big meet in January.

COACH: For you, crossing that finish line and beating your personal best at that meet would make all the mornings worth it.

KRISTIN: Yes. Yes, it would.

How Does MI Work?

No question, this athlete felt full of doubt and ambivalence. It's also clear that she and her coach seemed to trust each other. Let's look at how this coach used the athlete's language to help her develop and express her own reasons for changing. The coach went forward with the notion that Kristin had the motivation for her goals inside her and that she did not have to provide that for her. Instead of encouraging or inspiring, the coach looked for "change talk"—Kristin's own words that expressed her desire for success. We will define this in some detail shortly. Change talk emerged when Kristin said, "I do want to break my 60-meter time." Of course, she immediately followed with "but that probably means adding morning workouts." That's the ambivalence described in Chapter 1. Her coach did not focus on her reasons for *not* trying harder (getting out of bed) but instead focused on her change talk ("I want to break my 60-meter time").

> It's the change talk that comes from the athlete's own mouth that is important.

She might have felt a pull toward telling Kristin that getting out of bed was not such a problem for a healthy young woman (the righting reflex; see Chapter 2), but she was able to work to ignore that pull to fix. Instead, she used a listening statement that *rested on her change talk.* "You're not sure it's worth it. But a part of you is really focused on that 60-meter time. . . ."

When Kristin heard these words, they affirmed what she knew as true; she did not feel a need to argue back because she heard that her coach understood both her difficulty in practicing and her desire to be her best. What the coach said was accurate, and Kristin let her know this. The coach followed with the statement "You want to work at it." This brought forth a gold mine of motivation from Kristin. It's the change talk (positive personal motivations) that comes from the athlete's own mouth that is important, not the change talk that comes from the coach's mouth.

FROM THE FRONTLINE

Change talk that athletes express, especially if it has genuine emotion behind it, is a powerful motivator. Scientists studying MI have used audio recordings of conversations to analyze the impact of language on actual behavior change. They find that "less is more" when it comes to the behavior of the helper: if you hold back from solving challenges and making the case for change, and especially if you avoid confrontational language, and allow the person to speak for themselves about change, it impacts behavior change. The stronger the change talk, the better it predicts change. When we set the right tone in our conversations with athletes and gently strategize for the language we want them to be saying to themselves, we are cultivating change talk. MI is not a trick. It is more like practicing a sport; the more you practice MI, the better you will get at it and the more able you will be to help athletes even in the most difficult situations. That said, it isn't necessarily effective if athletes have already made up their minds *not* to work harder, or to be on time, or to cooperate with team members. MI works best when the athletes have the desire within them, but it has been sidelined by competing needs.

Ambivalence and Doubt Are Opportunities to Change

We mentioned that in the world of sports, MI is a relatively new approach, but it has been used in the world of public health, counseling, law enforcement, and medicine for three decades, with strong results. This is because people facing health challenges, addictions, and dangerous behaviors almost always feel two ways about their situation, what we call ambivalence. It is rare individuals who do not care at all about the harm they do to themselves with bad habits, although they do exist. Much more commonly, people feel two ways about their dilemma: they want to change, but they don't want to face the challenge of changing. As you may have recognized already, this is a normal part of the human condition. All of us would like to change in positive ways, but we fear and avoid the challenges that come with it. Yet we often have the resources within us to cope with that fear and avoidance even if it is packed away like a treasure in a dusty attic. This ambivalence, feeling two ways about something, can even occur after a long and extremely successful career. Take, for example, how full of joy *and* nostalgia Michael Jordan was as he retired from his legendary presence in the game of basketball.

When You Meet Resistance

Imagine the response from Kristin, the athlete, above, struggling with her sprint times, if the coach had said something like "It is probably a good idea if you wake up earlier for an extra practice each day." She would have argued back and heard herself say why this was no big deal. That won't motivate her to change, probably the opposite. Using MI, you avoid that kind of confrontation if you think it's likely to elicit a defensive reply. Herein lies the art of a conversation about change. How do you help people to speak more freely about their motivation to change? The first step is not to make things worse. A common refrain that some people use is "Don't just sit there, do something." Here, when talking to an athlete like Kristin who is struggling with doubt, it can be more beneficial to say to oneself, "Don't just do something, sit there."

We developed the phrase "rolling with resistance" to describe "rolling with" defensive statements such as "I'm fine. I can look after myself," by not arguing back or confronting the person. This is not a trick or clever strategy but simply an acknowledgment about how someone feels. Chapter 6 is devoted to this topic of rolling with resistance and dealing constructively with conflict in relationships with athletes.

Remembering the Mindset of a Guide

You'll notice not only the absence of pressure in the previous exchange with Kristin but also a purposeful, curious, and nonthreatening question that helped the player talk about her motivation. If that was like knocking on the door of change, now you are inside the house. As athletes juggle their desire to excel and balance it with their other needs and life demands, they navigate a confusing terrain. Here is where it is important to remember that using MI requires the willingness to take on the mindset and style of a guide.

THE LANGUAGE THEY USE

Paying attention to language is nothing new or particularly specialized, but a natural ability we have to "tune in" to exactly what others are saying. We have this capacity inside us, and it becomes noticeable and easier to work with as you get used to asking athletes to say in their own words how they feel about change. The change talk they use lifts their motivation to change (e.g., "I want to do it"), while another kind of language lowers it, the opposite of change talk (e.g., "I'm not sure I can succeed"). You might call this "counterchange talk" or even "stuck talk." You can also think of change talk and counterchange talk at two ends of a ruler, with a pointer that slides back and forth on it. At one end, the pointer is at the highest value of the ruler—that's where strong change talk sits. When we listen to athletes talking to us, we want to tune in to their language so we can tell which end of the ruler the pointer is on as the conversation goes along. This is because there is a special focus on how to respond to both change talk and the more negative "stuck talk."

Change talk can be hard to hear at first, especially if coaches have not practiced "listening for it." It is the language you hear that tells you the pointer is moving to the higher side of the ruler. If an athlete says, "I know I need to get to team practice on time, like everyone else," that is quite strong change talk. When you are listening intently, and you feel the pointer start moving upward, you are probably hearing change talk getting stronger. Listening for change talk is a natural human ability, and you might find, once you practice and tune your ear to it, that you have quite the knack for recognizing it.

You will also hear that negative "stuck talk" language, words that dampen the spirit ("I'm not sure I can do this"), deny the athlete's internal striving ("I don't even want to compete at this level in the first place"), give arguments against trying ("I'll never be as good as the rest of the team"), take away the value of the effort ("Who cares about a stupid track meet anyway?"), or emphasize the easy path ("It's just not worth getting up early 5 days a week"). Of course, all these things *might be true* in their experience. When athletes come to serious, thoughtful decisions that they do not want to train and compete, most coaches, while perhaps disappointed, can eventually accept their decisions. But what about when the athlete feels *both ways* about it? They will likely sound like this:

"I want to win, but it's not the end of the world if I don't."
"I hate the idea of getting out of bed at 5:00 A.M., but it's really not that bad when my friends are there too."
"This track meet is important because the college scouts are there, but in the end I don't really care about it."
"I'm good enough to be competing at this level, but maybe I'm not playing like it."

Does this sound familiar? It is the jail cell of doubt or uncertainty, when we feel two ways about something important to us. It is a normal state of mind, and an uncomfortable one, part of the process of striving, and it happens to almost everyone who achieves

Reflecting change talk important goals. Even though it is normal, this
can help athletes break uncertainty can trap athletes because they can't
free from doubt. move forward as their best selves when they are
experiencing it. It is like they are immobilized—
their energy is funneled into moving back and forth in their dilemma and not toward moving forward. MI is particularly useful when athletes are stuck in this kind of uncertainty because their own change talk language helps them move to one side of the dilemma and frees up the energy they need to break out of it.

The Importance of Hearing the Negative Side

Even though change talk is the primary focus of the coach when increasing motivation is the goal, it is important to remember that athletes will also offer those negative thoughts around feeling resigned, oppositional, or unwilling, as if they are saying, "I am willing to settle for things the way they are." As we know by now, this negative language is normal because it is one side of the underlying uncertainty about striving for anything, including excellence in sports. When we hear this language, it can be normal for us to want to push back or argue against it—this is the righting reflex. But the mindset of a guide allows a different approach. If you respond with *listening statements,* reflecting back what athletes are saying about their perspective, the athletes at least feel understood and some of the negative energy subsides. Here's an example, where we label the change talk, the stuck talk, and also the skill used by the coach that we address in the next chapter.

COACH: Danny, can I have a word with you? I'm noticing that this is the second time this week you've come late to practice. You missed your first drill each time.

DANNY: Well, everyone is late sometimes. [stuck talk]

COACH: It hasn't been easy for you to make it on time. [listening statement]

DANNY: I'm just about to flunk my Algebra class. Every single kid in there is smarter than I am. They ace the exams, and I can't get the work done in time. [stuck talk]

COACH: Your algebra class is taking up your energy right now, and it's hard to focus on anything else. [listening statement]

DANNY: Yes, it's getting so bad. I'm thinking of getting a tutor, like all the stupid kids do.

COACH: Math has become so stressful that it makes coming to practice on time a struggle right now. [listening statement]

DANNY: Yes! But I know I need to be here on time just like everyone else. [change talk]

COACH: In spite of all that's going on, you want to make the same commitment to these drills as your teammates. [listening statement]

DANNY: Yeah, I'll get it together. [change talk] I know I need to pull my weight here. [change talk] Even if I have to put in more time on the math . . . I don't want to let the swim team go. [change talk] Thanks, Coach.

them. Then the negative energy will subside. MI is most effective when you
allow yourself to feel that compassion for athletes.

HOW TO GET STARTED WITH MI

Here is how to get started with MI: Simply ask questions that will likely
lead to change talk. This is usually done with an open question, as in the
following examples:

"How would you like things to be different?"
"What changes are you considering?"
"What would be the best outcome, as you see it?"
"What have you already thought of?"
"What do you need the most in this situation?"

Of course, these questions will improve when you have details tailored
to your specific coaching situations, but in general, questions that ask for
envisioning of something different, something positive, are likely to pull
change talk when an athlete feels two ways about something. Let's return
for a moment to our conversation with Danny about being on time for
practice:

DANNY: I'm stressed about my schoolwork. I don't want to lose my
chance to play on the team by failing my classes. But I can't spend
all my time studying either, because then I don't get to practice
on time.

COACH: Hmm . . . Two very important things to you. What have you
thought about doing to balance things? [open question]

DANNY: Some of my friends have a tutor, so I've thought about seeing
if I can find one here on campus. [change talk]

Here's another example with a different athlete, Marcus:

MARCUS: I keep trying what you said, but I can't improve my time in
the freestyle.

COACH: What would be the ideal outcome here? What are you shooting for? [open questions]

If these questions open up talk about change, other techniques like listening statements can be used to keep things going. The interplay between questions and listening statements will be illustrated throughout this book.

MOVING PAST UNCERTAINTY

Uncertainly or doubt is surely not a problem to be ignored, removed, or blotted out of the minds of athletes but something to be acknowledged and worked through in a search for constructive solutions. The actor Jenson Ackles once said, "I used to be scared of uncertainty; now I get a high out of it." Of course, while you don't want to needlessly create fear and will want athletes to be focused and free of doubt, many a solid action plan emerges from a few moments of reflection. MI provides that space for the creative resolution of doubt.

Beyond all the details about MI and change talk, the conversation will look, sound, and feel like normal dialogue. When you harness an athlete's own good reasons to change, your job is to avoid taking credit for it. Then outcomes, like better performance, are likely to emerge. Later, in Part II of this book, we discuss the skills for making this happen.

ENJOY THE CONVERSATION

You might well get the impression that the use of MI is serious business, requiring an earnest and enquiring mind on your part. It does, but this does not mean the conversation has to be serious and "heavy." Indeed, the more you enjoy conversations about improvement and change, the more an athlete will. That's when real progress often happens in front of your eyes.

QUESTIONS TO CONSIDER

- What methods do you use to motivate athletes?
- What can you do to lift your own motivation?
- When you are really busy, how does this stress affect your conversations with athletes?

CHAPTER 4

Skills

Never discard listening as a source of learning.
It could be the most important decision you
ever make.
—RICHIE BENAUD, cricketer and commentator

HIGHLIGHTS

+ *Asking:* Be brief, encourage people to say what they think and feel, and open the door to talking about change.

+ *Listening:* Hear what the athlete is saying, and respond with a listening statement (empathy).

+ *Summarizing:* Gather the key points, especially the positive ones, present them, and check that they make sense.

+ *Mindset:* Have a relaxed but curious approach that is genuinely interested.

THE KICKOFF

If you have 60 seconds with a team or athlete, what conversation skills will you use to be at your best? What about a longer chat with a struggling player? Consider how you might respond to Hannah. She is a dedicated athlete, passionate about improving her performance. When you inquire how she is, you hear this: "I've been OK, yeah, thanks, but I didn't like what I saw out there in practice today. Some people have got to get their attitude right. I mean you should have seen the looks I got. Who wants to come in for practice with that sort of thing going on?"

Now what? Let's assume you want to connect and help her feel more settled and turn this setback around. What conversation skills will you bring to bear here? Are you going to ask her five or six closed (yes-or-no) questions all in a row? We doubt it. Imagine that kind of conversation. You will clearly want to use other skills, and what might they be?

As you know, Hannah is not alone. There are countless other daily challenges where you want to help in this way, such as with a player who can't seem to get over a recent poor performance, or another whom you want to say something to that might boost his motivation. To assist in that process, we'll review three core skills in this chapter:

1. *Asking*
2. *Listening*
3. *Summarizing*

For each skill, we will examine two uses in turn:

a. *The basics:* for improving your general communication
b. *When used in MI:* for when you are talking about change and improvement

To keep our feet on the ground, we will focus from time to time on that conversation with Hannah.

STRENGTHS LENSES ON?

We had our "strengths lenses" on when we described Hannah above as "dedicated" and "passionate." In other words, we saw her not just as an athlete with problems but as a person with strengths (see Chapter 2). It's well worth putting on these lenses when using MI to lift someone's motivation. Imagine a dull and gray world in which you only see problems to be solved, deficits to be corrected. We predict you will experience low motivation inside yourself and maybe even in athletes too. Optimism is important, and if focused on strengths it provides a wonderful platform for stoking the fire of motivation within athletes. Enjoyment matters.

SETTING THE PACE

Imagine you decide to head out after reading this chapter and try a few things out. You choose your moment, not a difficult challenge but one where you have an opportunity for a few quiet and informal minutes with an athlete. If you set off at a sprinter's pace, even your highest level of communication skill will be of little use. Some people become so excited about the power of an MI approach that they rush into their next conversation trying to do too much. Starting off "slow and steady" is a smart approach because this will give you time to make adjustments to your usual conversation routines. A couple of deep breaths before and during the conversation will keep your mindset clear and flexible. We talked in Chapter 2 about a calm heart and an uncluttered mind—here's where this guideline will serve you well.

SKILL 1: ASKING

Some questions have huge impact; others land with a thud. So what's the difference? Genuine curiosity in the first place is important. If you are going through the motions, distracted by something or even trying to be too clever, your question might not hit the mark.

Our approach to questions in MI is based on three key requirements. They should

1. Be brief and be followed by the use of other skills, such as listening statements and summaries.
2. Encourage people to express how they think and feel.
3. Open the door to using MI for talking about change and lifting motivation.

Asking a good question to begin is like knocking on someone's door. The initial knock needs to be respectful, clear, not too intrusive, and backed up by a willingness to connect. It is highly likely to be an open rather than closed question and ideally short and clear. There will be less focus on "I" and more on "you." You seldom knock on a door shouting out a long rambling sentence that ends " . . . and it's me here!" If the question is interesting, and relevant to them, they might invite you in!

The Basics

Open and Closed Questions

Closed questions usually invite a "yes" or "no" answer, while open ones leave it to the athlete to elaborate. In general, open questions begin with words like "What," "How," and "Why," where closed questions begin with words like "Are," "Do," and "Did." Focusing on asking more open questions is both a state of mind and a matter of technical proficiency. If you want to explore the athlete's views you will be better served by an open question than a closed one. An open question is an opportunity to explore, like a flag you are waving that identifies you as a coach who is interested in the players' perspective.

"Did you do the exercises I recommended?" says "I want an answer to this question."
"How did it go with those exercises I suggested?" says "I am interested in your progress and open to your thoughts about my strategies."

Take a look at the questions below, and see if you can identify which are open and which are closed. It may help you reflect on your own practice if you imagine you are the athlete being asked these questions. How might you respond to the two kinds of questions?

EXERCISE 4.1. Which is which—open (O) or closed (C)?

1. Did you think you played your best today? _____ O or _____ C
2. What did you like about how you played there? _____ O or _____ C
3. How is our morale as a team right now? _____ O or _____ C
4. Do we have players right now who are just in it for themselves? _____ O or _____ C
5. Did the referee call your foul? _____ O or _____ C
6. Are you planning to practice this weekend? _____ O or _____ C
7. What sort of plans do you have for practicing this weekend? _____ O or _____ C
8. Will you do some sprints between now and the next practice? _____ O or _____ C
9. What are your thoughts about sprints as a way to improve between now and next practice? _____ O or _____ C

The open questions are numbers 2, 3, 7, and 9.

Shorter Is Better

Consider how to reply to Hannah's outburst that ended "Who wants to come in for practice with that sort of thing going on?" In this situation we could come up with an open question using just two words, "What happened?" Often, being skillful means being simple. Consider the impact on Hannah of adding what we call "dribble" to the question, unnecessary words, or additional questions, such as this: "Can I ask you, one of the things I am wondering about, how did all this come about, or is it something you don't want to talk to me about now?" Two questions, not one, three unnecessary references to yourself, and you couldn't blame Hannah for wondering what to say next. It's confusing! Less is more in so many situations.

The Limitations of Questions

There's a tradition in sports coaching of using questions as the key skill, repeatedly. Consider for the moment what happens if you rely on *only* questions. In this example the coach is talking to an athlete just returning from an injury break:

> COACH: How are you today?
>
> ATHLETE: Good. I'm OK—not quite ready to go yet.
>
> COACH: What sort of practice have you been doing?
>
> ATHLETE: My usual, going OK.
>
> COACH: Where are you going to be after lunch?
>
> ATHLETE: Back around here for a while.
>
> COACH: Who's been working with you this week on those drills?
>
> ATHLETE: Mostly me alone because I know what to do. I have heard it so many times this week.
>
> COACH: Are you ready to head back into competition?

This conversation feels like a dance that never gets moving. There's not a lot wrong with any of the questions in themselves, yet the coach seems to drag the athlete this way and that, leaving her no time to answer any question in depth. She is a passive recipient of what probably feels like an investigation, and she is not trusted to provide wisdom at any point. It's hard on both parties. The coach is continually burdened with having to find the next question and is pulled into the role of what we call the "deficit detective," who searches out for things that are wrong to put right. Is this efficient use of time? Probably not. What's missing? Empathy for the athlete for a start, where the coach demonstrates that he or she is "listening." What that involves, which is much more than being quiet, we will address later in this chapter.

Should We Know the Answers to Questions We Ask?

Creative coaches sometimes ask questions they know the answer to, but they ask them so athletes can take ownership of the answer. This prevents you talking all the time and hands the baton over to the athlete to do some of the running. Then there's another kind of question, one that you choose carefully, that you don't know the answer to, because it's inside the athlete. This latter kind of question is what MI draws traction from, where you know what's important for the athlete to consider but you genuinely don't know what sense they will make of it.

Questions and MI

Questions with Movement

Questions used in the service of MI are *forward-looking* and involve asking athletes to say for themselves how and why they might change. An open question is the easiest and most direct way to get this kind of conversation started. You don't know the answer to these questions, but together you search for it. What does change look like as seen through their eyes? Notice the difference between "How are you?" and "How might you make these practice sessions more helpful?" Both are open questions, both are perfectly acceptable, but only the second is about change. One is stationary, the other has movement.

> Ask athletes to say how and why they might change.

EXERCISE 4.2. Which questions focus on change?

Here's a list of eight questions, five of which focus on change (C) and others that don't (NC, for no change). Can you spot them?

1. What thoughts do you have about practice for this week? _____ C or _____ NC
2. Have you purchased your helmet yet? _____ C or _____ NC
3. How important is it to you to get on better with other players? _____ C or _____ NC
4. How do you see your game progressing over the next few weeks? _____ C or _____ NC
5. When did you start playing? _____ C or _____ NC
6. Have you always been a team player? _____ C or _____ NC
7. What will it take for you to get over this injury? _____ C or _____ NC
8. How confident are you that you will get on top of this challenge? _____ C or _____ NC

The questions focusing on change are numbers 1, 3, 4, 7, and 8.

Curiosity about Motivation and Change

The moment you ask a curious, open question about change, motivation raises its head and change talk will emerge. It's an opportunity to encourage and build momentum. You are not going to solve any problems for athletes but rather, gently, guide them in a positive direction. The most powerful tool for doing this is listening.

SKILL 2: LISTENING

If your question to Hannah about that unhappy practice session ("What happened?") was like knocking on a door, listening is what you do when you go inside, when you get a chance to express empathy to promote behavior change. It's an active process involving you making short summary statements that help her to clarify further. This listening starts with you wondering what's going on for her, and it's a skill you can get better at through practice in everyday conversation, not unlike giving exercise to an empathy "muscle." You can even go online and flex this muscle by looking at a video of people in a hospital (search for "Cleveland Clinic Video").

EXERCISE 4.3. Just imagine: Empathy in action.

Consider the following scene: You walk into the locker room to find all your players there getting ready for the game, with the exception of Ralph, one of your most important players. As game time approaches you begin to get nervous. You call and text Ralph, but his phone goes to voice mail. You are forced to take the field, and as you do you catch Ralph walking into the locker room and slowly putting on his uniform. He's more than 2 hours late.

How do you feel? What is your orientation toward Ralph right now? If you are like us, you might feel frustration and confusion.

Here's his back story: He woke up ready for the game. He went through some extra practice and game review at his house. On his way to the stadium, he realized that his phone hadn't charged properly. He thought it was OK as he would be in the locker room in 15 minutes and could plug it in. Besides, he usually turned his phone off during the games anyway. About 5 minutes before he arrived at the stadium, his mother called him. She had fallen down in her apartment. Without thinking about it, Ralph turned his car around and raced over to his mother's house. When he got there, an ambulance was on the scene. His mother was stable, but they thought she might have broken her hip. Ralph went to call his coach, but his phone was dead. The ambulance driver said they needed to go to the hospital. Ralph followed the ambulance to the hospital and got his mother a bed to be evaluated. He then tried to call a couple of his coaches, but all his calls went to voice mail.

What are your feelings toward Ralph now? Probably more understanding of his behavior and situation. All of our players have stories. They have reasons not to comply with rules, reasons to resist. By asking open questions and listening to them, we have more access to information about them that will help us both empathize and build trust and common ground so we can more accurately and effectively guide and fix.

In this section, we cover the basics first and then turn to how listening can be used in MI to lift motivation. You can find a quick reference tool in Part IV called "Empathy: Becoming a Better Coach."

FROM THE FRONTLINE

We know a legendary international soccer player who looks back on his career and points to a single moment that seemed to change everything for him, when his coach noticed he was very low on confidence. It had been going on a while. The coach put a hand on his shoulder and invited him to go for a walk. It wasn't a question that was asked, more a statement: "You're not yourself these days, and it looks like you are struggling." The conversation that followed was a turning point, and a new path opened up. MI provides a framework for making choices about what skill to use, when, and for what purpose. Listening statements—the expression of the empathy you feel—can be very powerful.

The Basics

Broken down into its component parts, listening involves at least a two-phase sequence: one is an internal experience that you have; the other is external, something you say to the athlete.

Hearing

Hearing involves something like getting into a zone, not unlike that of an athlete in a state of calm attentiveness, free of distracting mental chatter. Or how we, as coaches, might watch a game, both taking it in on every level and having a sense of what might happen next. However, in this case the zone has a special quality: it is infused with curiosity and empathy, imagining the experience of another. When in this zone, we can hear lots of things. The challenge is to log them and decide what's important, because we will be selecting and responding in the second phase of listening. By watching and listening to the person you are talking to with the same attention and care that you would watch a game, you will notice new opportunities to connect.

Consider again Hannah's reply to your initial query, which falls on you like a shower of mixed feelings: "I've been OK, yeah, thanks, but I didn't like what I saw out there in practice today. Some people have got to get their attitude right. I mean you should have seen the looks I got." She said quite a lot. Imagine it's a video being played. What image strikes you as most important? Or, if you imagine hanging up the topics on pegs in your mind, or on a mental cork board, what are these, and which are the most important? You'll want to get an idea of this because, having heard what she said, you need to decide what to offer her by way of reply. You'll be making a guess about what she means, and over time you get better at doing this. Here are some possibilities:

- Hannah isn't feeling OK.
- She is disappointed in some of her teammates.
- She didn't like what happened in practice.
- She didn't have a good practice session.
- Colleagues looked at Hanna in a way she didn't like.

Making a Listening Statement

In the second phase of listening, you offer a short summary by way of reply, a guess, or an attempt to "capture the core" of her experience. This is you expressing empathy. If your hunch is that she wasn't happy with what happened in practice, you could simply offer up a statement such as "You just didn't like what happened out there today."

This is a critical moment. By offering a listening statement, you are again raising the flag that she is important to you, showing you care and building trust. She will notice your effort to connect and will elaborate or even correct you if your guess was not quite right. A connection is being formed between the two of you, based on your effort to empathize with her, to imagine her experience.

> At the heart of listening lies a space to wonder.

When we say that connection and communication are important in coaching, we are talking about the moments in which this type of empathy and understanding are demonstrated. You will probably feel a little hesitant as you make the statement and hand the conversation baton over to her, probably wondering, "Have I got this right?" or "How will this land with her?" Our best advice here is to let her take the baton and try not to interrupt or take over the conversation. The space for you both to wonder lies at the heart of listening.

Here's how the exchange with Hannah might continue, with the coach offering the initial listening statement about her not liking what happened in practice, followed by three more listening statements:

COACH: You just didn't like it out there today. [listening statement]

HANNAH: No, I didn't. It was disrespectful in my book.

COACH: They looked at you in a way you didn't like. [listening statement]

HANNAH: Well, exactly. I was trying to keep focused on my own routine, and it was like, "Hey look at her, she's at it with that wacky stuff again." They didn't say that, but this is the look I got.

COACH: They found your warm-up routine sort of amusing. [listening statement—which turns out to be not quite accurate]

HANNAH: No, I don't think they thought it was funny; it's just not what they would do, and I also think they are jealous. They must be.

COACH: And this distracted you when you least needed it. [listening statement]

HANNAH: You got it. Why do I have to put up with that?

The coach used a skill that takes the conversation forward in a natural and seemingly effortless way. It was time efficient too.

"You got it" from Hannah tells the coach that she feels understood. One open question followed by a series of listening statements were the only skills used. You might find it useful to think about this a bit like a musical score. If you use abbreviations (O = open question; L = listening statement), the above coach's skills would look something like this: O, L, L, L, L. The four statements from the coach got closer to how Hannah feels, more quickly, than if she had been asked a series of questions. Chapter 8, on rapid connecting, describes how to do this in all kinds of everyday situations. Listening in this way improves the connection and the relationship with every statement. It also takes pressure off you because you don't have to find the next question, let alone the solution, because the athlete will. When the athletes generate the ideas, they are more likely to be motivated and committed to moving forward. An accurate listening statement is like a thank-you note—it improves connection. You can find an easy-access quick reference tool in the MI Playbook (Part IV of this book): "Listening: Getting the Basics Right."

At a basic level, a following style governs the use of listening statements. Your aim is simply to understand and help athletes to say what they think and feel, regardless of the subject. At a more advanced level, which we turn

> A listening statement takes the pressure off you to find the next question.

to next, a guiding style governs the use of listening statements, where coaches use them to steer the athletes' attention to exploring change and improvement. That's when you are harnessing the all-important change talk.

Listening and MI

The moment you turn the conversation toward change, MI comes to the fore—empathy and listening statements are used in the service of clarifying the path ahead. Returning to that conversation with Hannah, how are you going to steer her toward a plan of action? How is she going to handle those fellow athletes? Ignore them? Have a chat with them? Who knows best, you or Hannah? Jointly, we suspect, you can find the answer. This is when you will be using MI and looking out for the change talk we described in the last chapter. Here's a hint—it's already there when we know where to look.

Listen with a Focus on Change Talk

Here's a sample of what might take place with Hannah. An open question starts the ball rolling; then consider what happens next:

COACH: What's going to help you get back to practice feeling really focused tomorrow?

HANNAH: I just can't see it with those guys around.

COACH: It's hard to imagine. [listening statement]

HANNAH: No. I can *imagine* it, [change talk] but it's hard to make it happen.

COACH: How might you do this? [calling for more change talk]

HANNAH: I'm down right now coach, to be honest. What I need to do is have a conversation or two with them. [change talk] Hard to imagine. I know it's a good idea, [change talk] but I'm not sure I have it in me.

COACH: It might be hard, but you want to do it. [listening statement]

HANNAH: I'm going to have a good rest tonight, and tomorrow I think it might happen. [change talk]

COACH: You are going to recharge so you can make this happen. [listening statement]

HANNAH: Yes, it's up to me, and I'm going to do it [stronger change talk] and then get on with life.

The more Hannah hears herself talking about change, the more likely she will be to step out and do it. Listening was used to give her the space to think it through, and critically, it was focused on the change talk, to encourage her to say what she wanted to do and come to a decision that she owned. She will be more motivated by that which makes sense to her, deep down. After just a couple of minutes spent asking a useful question or two about change and listening in this active way, Hannah's motivation and her resolve to change, has been strengthened.

Dominated by the Righting Reflex?

Hannah would not have taken ownership of decisions if the coach had succumbed to the righting reflex and simply told her what she might do. Reinforcing the message about the righting reflex, here's what that conversation might have looked like (don't use it because it will use you!):

HANNAH: I've been OK, yeah, thanks, but I didn't like what I saw out there in practice today. Some people have got to get their attitude right. I mean you should have seen the looks I got.

COACH: How about I come to practice with you tomorrow to give you some support.

HANNAH: Hey thanks, appreciate it, but what difference would that make? They would just think, *Oh, she's gone and complained to the coach.* It could make it worse . . .

COACH: Well, then, maybe we agree to sit down and have a word together, all of us.

HANNAH: OK, thanks. I'll think about it and let you know, OK?

COACH: Anytime, just ask. OK, Hannah?

The coach certainly feels concern and has lots of bright ideas, but they are his ideas, not Hannah's. That's not in itself unhelpful for the coach to produce ideas that might work. However, to impose them on Hannah without first listening to hers is where the righting reflex comes unstuck. Offering advice is one thing; ignoring the athlete's wisdom is another altogether.

SKILL 3: SUMMARIZING

Can you recall what an athlete has said that's important? How well have you listened? Summarizing brings together what's been said in a conversation, or a segment of it, as accurately as you can, for the benefit of the athlete. It's not necessary in a very short conversation, but in a longer one it's a technique with huge potential. It also allows you to shift the focus of the conversation, with the athlete on board, or bring it to an end.

The Basics

What do you make of these two summaries offered to Hannah?

Summary A

"So those fellow athletes got on your nerves, and I don't blame you really and maybe you overreacted a bit. It sounds like they were maybe trying to put you off or be better than you. Anyway, I suggest you sleep on it and let's see if I can come with you to practice tomorrow, OK?"

Summary B

"Can I just make sure I got what you've said, OK? [Pauses, waits, Hannah nods her agreement] You set out to go through your best preparation routine, and you are concerned about the way those fellow athletes looked at you during your warm-up. They distracted you, it felt disrespectful, and you think they might be jealous of you. What you feel quite determined to do is get back there tomorrow, have a conversation with them, and then move on."

If a summary brings together what the athlete has actually said and feels, then Summary B is by some distance the more accurate and effective. Summary A violated the principles of good practice on a number of fronts. The coach passes judgment ("maybe you overreacted a bit"), offers his own interpretation ("It sounds like they were maybe trying to put you off"), and gives advice about how to solve the problem ("Let's see if I can come with you to practice tomorrow"). What you are aiming for is an accurate summary of what the athlete said and felt. Your views are secondary at this stage. By keeping closely to athletes' experience, they feel understood and your relationship is improved; a summary can also confirm and reinforce whatever decisions the athlete made about improving things.

When you hand a summary over to athletes, your goal is to ensure they say something like "Yes, that's exactly right; you got me." So how do you do it?

Focus on the Athlete

If your focus is only on what the athlete has said, you can leave out quite a few things from the summary, such as attempts to solve a problem, give advice, state an opinion, or pass judgment. It's not about "I," the coach, what you think, but about "you," the person and athlete, ideally embracing his or her dreams, strengths, and how he or she wants to improve things.

Introduce the Summary

An introduction, which can also contain an element of permission-asking, allows you both momentarily to step back from the conversation and alerts someone like Hannah to monitor the accuracy of your effort. "Sorry to interrupt; you've said a lot, and I just want to make sure I'm getting it all"; or "Can I make sure I've got you so far?"

Capture the Core

A summary is a set of statements you make that captures the core of what's been said and felt by the athlete. Since you can't simply repeat everything, what do you select for putting in a summary? It's your choice; what you include can and will affect the athlete for better or worse. Our advice is to make sure you focus on the person, not just the athlete, and that you don't forget to include references to his or her strengths, effort, and aspirations, an illustration of which is contained above in the very first part of the summary offered to Hannah: "You set out to go through your best preparation routine. . . ."

Choose Your Words with Care

Among the markers of skillfulness in a summary is the use of "you" rather than "I"; if you can pay careful attention to the exact words used during the conversation, try to use them again in the summary. A skillful summary is a lean offering that can be absorbed with ease by the athlete.

> In a summary, use the athlete's own words.

Check Back with the Athlete

By watching the person carefully after your summary, you can usually tell how it landed. Often they are shocked that you just "mind read" them. If you're unsure about how your summary was received or you have the sense there is still more, say just a few words at the end of the summary to ensure that the athlete has the opportunity to correct or confirm what's been said; for example: "What have I missed?" It can be worthwhile for you to pause at this point because people often say how they really want to move forward, exactly the kind of change talk that MI is tuned into.

Summarizing and MI

Imagine a summary that contains the positive highlights, that gathers together all the change talk that an athlete has used. That's an MI-inspired summary, like handing back to athletes their own stated good reasons to change. The logic is this: They would have heard themselves express change talk during the conversation; they might have also heard you restate the change talk when you offered your listening statements; and now, in the summary, they hear it once again, powerful reminders and expressions of their motivation to change. As we noted above, a summary is a great opportunity to confirm and reinforce whatever decisions athletes made about improving things. What you often hear in reply is even stronger change talk that confirms the resolution to change, something like "Yes, that's right, I'm going to head out and do it." That will help you both to move forward. A quick reference handout, "Summaries," can be found in Part IV.

QUESTIONS TO CONSIDER

- When you ask questions of an athlete, how often do you *not* know the answer ahead of time?
- In conversations with players, what percentage of the time are you talking, versus the athlete talking?
- How can you train yourself to notice what's going on in conversations?

CHAPTER 5

Affirming

When you're that young, it doesn't take
a lot to be encouraged, or discouraged . . .
they raised my game . . . they saw
something in me I didn't see in myself.
— SIR KEN ROBINSON, educationalist

HIGHLIGHTS

+ Praise, while offered with good intentions, is a judgment
  handed down in the hope that it will stoke the fire of
  motivation. It can easily be overused.
+ Affirmation is less of a judgment, more of an appreciation of
  positive qualities and behaviors that you notice. It is more
  likely to lift motivation and inspire further achievement.
+ Affirmation can even be used when things are not going well.

THE KICKOFF

Who says coaching is easy? What works well for one athlete doesn't work
for another. Hence the toolbox idea, and in this chapter we look at two
skills in particular: praise and affirmation. Our advice is to use praise with
care, not like confetti, and to sharpen your use of affirmation because it
has a more powerful effect on your relationship and on building a "can-do"
attitude in athletes.

How can the use of praise cut across an athlete's natural desire to be creative on the field of play? We suspect that with James it was probably used alongside the *righting reflex* (see Chapter 1) where, without even thinking about it, his coaches might have solved problems *for* him and used praise as a sweetener. Here's an imaginary example:

COACH: Well done; that was getting better. [praise]

JAMES: It felt better; thanks.

COACH: I tell you what to do now. Try again, only this time . . . (*Explains what to do.*)

JAMES: Yes, OK. (*Tries again, only this time he fails.*)

COACH: OK, don't worry; you are doing fine [praise]. Let me show you what went wrong . . . (*Explains what went wrong. James looks up, waiting for instruction . . . maybe praise too.*) OK, well done; let's try again, only this time. . . .

It's not that these comments from the coach are way off base. The athlete seems to appreciate the optimism and enthusiasm. Yet the driver of learning seems to be not the athlete but the coach, who becomes the "deficit detective," correcting what's wrong and using praise to lift motivation. If that cycle were to be repeated four or five times a session, what effect will it have on learning? Will it lead to the kind of dependence James talks about ("I stopped thinking and started conforming")? You will notice a similar pattern unfolding with teams, for example, when a coach says something like "Great practice. We need to see that energy in the game this time."

The question is, does this necessarily raise motivation and improve performance?

PRAISING AND AFFIRMING: WHAT'S THE DIFFERENCE?

What do you make of these two efforts to encourage an athlete?

1. *Praise:* "Well done, you used the gaps in their defense really well today. Keep up the good work."
2. *Affirmation:* "You somehow saw the gaps in their defense today."

Consider what the athlete will say next. The first effort (praise) might be met with "Thank you, Coach," and hopefully with a glow of pride too. The conversation might stop there. Dependence on further praise might develop, and this is what James experienced as unhelpful. The second offering (affirmation) has a different effect, and it's more of an invitation to talk more. The athlete will look not outward for confirmation of learning but inward toward how it came about. The response might well be something like, "Yes, I decided not to rush too much, and time sort of stood still." There, in that instant, the athlete is discovering what will make for better performance next time.

We met a hockey player who had a very clear recollection of what seemed to us like the natural use of affirmation by her coach: She said, "I was really down about how I played, but one thing he said really hit me as I struggled to regain form. He just said, 'You tried your guts out there today and seemed to have so much courage.' It hit me between the eyes. He was right. It wasn't all bad." Affirmations help athletes to encourage themselves. Put simply, with praise the learning is driven from the outside, while with affirmation the learning is driven from the inside.

EXERCISE 5.1. Spot the difference.

See if you can spot which statement is praise and which is affirmation (answers are below). There is sometimes a gray area when it's difficult to tell the difference, but with practice you will spot an affirmation by the reaction of the athlete you are speaking with. Put another way, as a colleague put it, it's not cleverness that will drive your skill acquisition but being guided by how athletes respond.

1. "That must have taken some real strength to play both games today."
2. "I liked that shot; well done."
3. "Nice work. Keep after it!"

4. "You seemed to keep your composure when under pressure."
5. "You found a way to really focus out there even with the weather."
6. "I thought that was a great game you had today; well done."
7. "There's your honesty again, in that meeting."
8. "Nice work out there."

Praise was involved in numbers 2, 3, 6, and 8. Numbers 1, 4, 5, and 7 were affirmations, where the coach pointed out an observable detail in the athlete's attitude or behavior. We suspect you are already using affirming to some degree, so our aim here is to sharpen your understanding and encourage you to practice and reap the rewards of your effort. One way of describing the difference is that praise is an external judgment while affirmation is an observation of what's there for the athlete to take ownership of. You praise an athlete; you affirm a person.

Our experience in using MI is that affirmation is a more powerful driver of motivation, self-discovery, and a "can-do" attitude than is praise. This is not to suggest that praise has no value. Indeed, toward the end of this chapter we will examine some guidelines from research about what to focus your use of praise on.

> Affirmations help athletes to encourage themselves.

FROM THE FRONTLINE

When I first learned the difference between praise and affirmation, I thought I'd give it a go to help empower the young soccer players that I coach. Praise is widespread in sports, and if affirmations have a more positive effect on the athletes than praise, then why not use affirmations instead? When standing on the touchline, "great pass" [praise] could become "that's vision to see that pass!"; or "good dribble" [praise] becomes "you keep composed even under pressure." I've noticed this helps to improve the performance of other athletes, not just the one you've affirmed—they try to replicate the "vision" or "composure" shown by the affirmed player.

—DIMITIR PERSEY, soccer coach

When affirming, you are more a curious and admiring witness to what you observe than the arbiter or judge of what you want to see in your athletes.

THE EXPERIENCE OF AFFIRMATION

How would you feel to be at the receiving end of each of the affirmations below? What might you say in reply?

EXERCISE 5.2. If you were at the receiving end.

"That was some attack they had. You weathered that onslaught like a gladiator."

"I see how mad you are. You care about the team and getting this right."

"You noticed her coming and you somehow found a way to slip around. . . ."

"You really want to put the effort in, even though there are ups and downs."

Notice how the above statements encourage you to say more about your strengths and motivation. In each example, your reply would focus on your hopes, self-belief, and a "can-do" attitude toward better performance. What is this experience like in conversation?

EXERCISE 5.3. Feel the difference.

A 17-year-old soccer player in a tense game situation produces a long, low pass that dissects a defense and leads to a wonderful outcome, an act of daring and creativity seemingly beyond his age. Imagine meeting him after the game, with a desire to focus on that pass and to encourage him to develop further. What might you say, and why? The first exchange (A) involves praise, the second (B) affirmation:

A: Praising

COACH: Looking good out there today; that was a hell of a play! Well done. [praise]

PLAYER: Thanks coach. (*Smiles.*)

COACH: That's one of the best I've seen out of you this year. It will be good to see more of those. [praise]

PLAYER: Sure, thanks.

COACH: Rest up and let's see more of that next week, OK?

B: Affirming

COACH: That long pass—it seemed like you paused and had the vision to see that gap in their defense. [affirmation]

PLAYER: Yeah, it felt like time stood still. (*Smiles.*)

COACH: In that moment you found that confidence of yours to just go for it. [affirmation]

PLAYER: Yeah, I just acted on my gut, but my mind was super clear too.

COACH: You found a way to trust yourself in a big moment. [affirmation]

PLAYER: Yeah, I want to trust it more next time. You know? [change talk]

Affirming is acknowledging something inside the player that's already there, which cannot be taken away, like shining a light on something positive that you've noticed. Over time they get to rely less on your judgment and more on their qualities, strengths, or evidence of them that you point out to them. In doing all this, you will notice that affirmation strengthens your relationship with the player almost beyond measure.

GETTING GOING

Wear the Strengths Lenses

Earlier in the book we used the idea of putting on a set of lenses through which you can see people's strengths (Chapter 2). The more you look through them, the more you will see, and the verbal delivery of an affirmation will be straightforward.

A coach who says something like, "You keep composed even under pressure" just noticed something on the spot and offered the affirmation. It can be done from the side of the field just as easily as it can be to offer praise.

The more we affirm, the easier it is for athletes to accept our constructive criticism or advice. That is because they will see our advice in the context of the idea that we fundamentally value them as a person. When we affirm, we raise that flag again about what kind of coach we are. By affirming, we are once again letting an athlete know that we fundamentally see them as good enough already, not flawed and unacceptable as people until they make a certain adjustment. It's the "love" part of "tough love." Without affirmation, we are just tough, and that diminishes trust and buy-in with players.

> Affirmation strengthens your relationship with the player.

The mentally distracting habit of always looking for faults is so powerful that this shift to focusing on strengths takes some getting used to. In time, it feels easier and the affirmations start to emerge quite naturally. The adjustment required is a bit like a slight shift in the position of your hand on a tennis racket, one that could make a big difference to the outcome. In time, it does.

Notice the Strengths

When you have time to just observe athletes, what are you looking at or for? You will quite rightly be noticing things that go wrong, but what about the positive things that also make a difference? This is where you can prepare yourself for using affirmation.

What qualities and strengths are driving the athletes you observe? Everyone is different, and even one individual will be using some qualities at one moment, others the next. A curious mindset will lead you to notice all kinds of things, some of which you might choose in the right moment to point out to athletes by using an affirmation, even during the action.

Table 5.1 lists the strengths you might look for in your athletes that can serve as the foundation for making an affirmation.

Spend a few moments scanning this list, and you will likely come up with some more adjectives. The next questions is, when you notice these strengths are expressed in their effort or behavior, how do you actually make the affirmation?

Ask about Strengths

A very direct route to making an affirmation is simply to ask athletes about their strengths. Then when they start talking about them, you can offer an affirmation by way of reply, like this:

COACH: How did you do that so well? [open question]

ATHLETE: I don't know, it seems like I just stopped thinking and did it.

COACH: You found a way to quiet your mind and really focus. [affirmation]

ATHLETE: Yes, exactly. I found this zone in my mind that was peaceful, and I felt really strong.

COACH: Makes me wonder how you might use this ability again.

ATHLETE: I need to worry less about the outcome I guess . . . to stop overthinking like I did in that game. [change talk]

TABLE 5.1. Strengths

• Accurate	• Organized	• Resilient
• Good communicator	• Creative	• Efficient
• Flexible	• Motivated	• Positive
• Lively	• Controlled	• Calm
• Adventurous	• Generous	• Honest
• Ambitious	• Brave	• Fair
• Good vision	• Authentic	• Assertive
• Focused	• Selfless	• Respectful
• Persevering	• Flexible	• Caring
• Good tactical thinking	• Diligent	

That curious open question encouraged the athlete to name the strength and opened the way for using an affirmation ("You found a way to quiet your mind and really focus") by way of reply. With the strengths lenses on, other similar questions will soon come to mind, such as "What are your greatest strengths as a hitter?" or "How have you managed to overcome so many challenges over the years?"

Self-Affirmations

If you ask athletes about what's important to them, or about the strengths they bring to their sport, they often make what is a "self-affirmation" in reply.

> COACH: How did you do that?
>
> ATHLETE: I just kept going and dug really deep. [self-affirmation]

There's a body of psychological research that confirms the positive impact of self-affirmation on attitude and behavior (Cohen & Sherman, 2014). This usually involves asking people to write down their most important values. However, in the world of everyday sporting conversation, you can simply ask athletes a question, the answer to which is self-affirmation. If their reply is a bit vague, you can then return to providing affirmations yourself.

> "What is it about this sport that you like so much?"
> "How did that work so well for you?"
> "In what way is this change in technique helping you?"

DELIVERING AN AFFIRMATION

An affirmation is not a question but a statement. Here's how to construct one.

EXERCISE 5.4. Construct an affirmation.

Consider this exchange with an athlete:

> ATHLETE: Wow that was tough, but I came through.
>
> YOUR RESPONSE: Somehow you found that extra gear to pull it off in that last quarter with the last drive. [affirmation]
>
> ATHLETE: (Looking bright) Yeah, I didn't know I had it; it just appeared. That feels really good now.

You want your comment to be more of a description, less of a compliment. Using the word *I* will make it feel more of a compliment, a judgment of yours. That's why it's best to start with the word *you* instead—for example: "You value . . . ," "You're really good at . . . ," "You're a person who . . . ," "You care about . . . ," "You're so . . . ," or "That must make you feel. . . ."

Try these three examples for yourself. How might you affirm the athlete?

Athlete makes a big play.

Your affirmation: _____

Our suggestion: "Courage and commitment there—quite something to see!"

ATHLETE: "I want to do better in this team."

Your affirmation: _____

Our suggestion: "You are the kind of player that is determined to contribute here."

ATHLETE: "I've got no gas in the tank."

Your affirmation: _____

Our suggestion: "You found a way to reach down deep and get it done!"

Observe and Follow-Up

What effect did your affirmation have? Usually, because the athlete continues talking, you have time to observe and to wonder what to say next. The illustrated scenario to end this chapter will bring to life how affirmation fits into an MI-inspired conversation that improves a "can-do" attitude.

If you really want to get on top of this skill, take a little time to write down a few lines about an athlete, even if most of your words are about their troubles and struggles. Then step back and ask yourself, "What does this story say about this athlete's strengths?" or "How does this strength help him or her?" Write down the strengths and how they might be of help. Then try to form an affirmation by gathering these key points together in a short sentence statement, using the word *you* rather than *me* or *I*.

EXERCISE 5.5. Transform praise into affirmation.

Consider how you might transform praise into affirmation. Take this example: "Well done. I'm impressed with your work today." Here's how to make the transformation: Imagine what positive qualities might have been needed to do the work involved. With those strengths lenses on, what do you see? Imagine one answer being "determination." Then here's the affirmation: "You've seemed determined to get the job done today." Here are two more common coaching examples:

Praise: "I liked what I saw today; nicely done."

Affirmation: "You had that look in your eye today, full of commitment."

Praise: "That was a good clean pass; well done."

Affirmation: "You somehow seem to spot these gaps for clean passing."

Now try these next examples for yourself:

Praise: "Well done; good running there."

Your affirmation: _

Our suggestion: "You seemed to dig deep and find that extra gear."

Praise: "That's the best I've seen you play; good stuff."

Your affirmation: _

Our suggestion: "You found your way to your high-level stuff out there today."

EXERCISE 5.6. Affirm in the face of failure.

A poor outcome might be disappointing, but it only tells half the story. Not everything was poor. Indeed, if you take luck and circumstance into account, athletes and teams can do really well, and fail. We often try to separate process from outcome in sports. Affirmations naturally do that. When we affirm, we are pointing out what is good about a person or athlete despite the results of a particular play or game. In that way, we are reinforcing positive traits and processes that should eventually lead to positive results and wins.

Affirmation can help here to refocus attention in the face of failure and to instill hope and the courage to continue. Notice how you can't make these affirmations if you don't have those "strengths lenses" on. Here are three examples:

Example 1

ATHLETE: I messed up, I know that.

YOU: You put your back into it, and you are the kind of player that can reflect on your performance.

Example 2

ATHLETE: Just because the position suits him doesn't mean it will suit me.

YOU: You know your strengths, and this game is important enough to you to figure out how you may or may not fit into this role.

Example 3

ATHLETE: Damn! I am fed up. This is the third time I have tried, and I've failed every time.

YOU: Your determination is what has had you sticking with it to get this right.

Affirming when things don't go well does not mean you ignore or bypass the way an athlete feels about an experience of failure. Rather, by highlighting strengths, you lay down a foundation that will give the athlete the courage and determination to explore new solutions and try again. It's a way of showing appreciation while keeping the athletes themselves at the center of the conversation. Indeed, the effect is to help them appreciate themselves, despite whatever setbacks are happening around them.

IN EVERYDAY SITUATIONS

While affirming is a communication skill, the technique is not an end in itself but a route to improving your relationship and continuing the conversation that helps athletes to see their potential and to act on it. When they sense your attitude, they respond more positively.

Of course, like any tool, the use of affirming needs to fit its purpose and not be overused. This is especially true as athletes become more veteran. They can become more sensitive to excessive use of affirmation. As a colleague remarked, "Don't affirm folks for breathing—it angers them" (Rosengren, 2018, p. 63).

> Affirming needs to fit its purpose.

Two Conversations

The examples below come from two very different ends of the sporting spectrum: elite performance and community engagement. What unites them is the way MI and affirmation are used to bring the best out of people learning to be the best they can be.

A Moment of Calm with an Elite Athlete

ATHLETE: Man, that was great.

COACH: (*Smiles.*) You found what it takes. [affirming]

ATHLETE: Yes! I must have.

COACH: Something came alive in you. [affirming]

ATHLETE: It was like a voice inside, very focused, showing me the way ahead. [self-affirmation]

COACH: What did it say?

ATHLETE: I don't know but something like "push, push!" (*Smiles.*)

COACH: Pure focus, and that voice led the way. [affirming]

ATHLETE: Yes, that's just how it felt. Maybe I can do even better. [change talk]

COACH: Using that voice again.

ATHLETE: Let it maybe get louder and stronger. [change talk]

A Talented Single Parent Considers Joining
a Recreational Team

COACH: How was that practice session for you?

PLAYER: Not bad . . . I found it difficult to be honest. Everything was too new.

COACH: You found a way to jump in there and see how it went. [affirmation]

PLAYER: Yes, exactly. I did OK, but I'm not sure about whether to come back to be honest.

COACH: You made the commitment today. [affirmation]

PLAYER: Yes, it was quite an effort to get childcare figured out, so I am happy I came.

COACH: So you managed to take that first step [affirmation] and meet a few of the other players too.

PLAYER: Yes, people here are friendly enough, which was nice.

COACH: I wonder what will help you to come back? We could help you with a lift, or even give you a special solo practice session; it's up to you.

PLAYER: Maybe next week I could have a little practice with you? [change talk]

In Teams

Affirmation has its place in helping teams. When we affirm a team, we reinforce what we observe on or around the field. We see it, we say it, and low and behold, it happens more frequently and autonomously. This can apply to things like collaboration, togetherness, and other aspects of team behavior that positively affect group dynamics and behavior.

Here are some examples of affirmations we have heard from dynamic coaches across various levels of amateur and professional sports competition:

"That fourth quarter was one in which many teams give up. You guys hung in there and stayed focused."

"There it is again, that grit. I saw you all fight today playing for each play."

"When you guys huddled up at the beginning of the game, you could tell by the way you communicated and looked at each other it was a band of brothers."

"You've got something to enjoy today, not just your win, your ability to get it done, but also your trust in each other. That was a team game you played."

PRAISE, GRATITUDE, AND AFFIRMATION: A CLOSER LOOK

Praise

"Be positive"! That's one piece of advice you pick up in all corners of sports. Findings from research in education suggest that you do better to praise things like effort, strategy, and perseverance rather than talent, ability, or intelligence (Dweck, 2017). It might not be helpful if your motive is mainly to make the player (or yourself!) feel better. It doesn't necessarily strengthen your relationship with an athlete. As one commentator noted, if your relationship is a strong one, you won't need it, and if it's a weak one, praise won't help much (Kohn, 2001).

The research on praise contains some surprising findings: There's an assumption that it's a reward—it is—and that it motivates better performance—it doesn't. Moreover, children who receive lavish praise are apparently more tentative and less likely to persist with complex tasks. Put bluntly, it can make them unhappy and less creative (see Hattie & Timperley, 2007). Is this why we notice some successful coaches being much more restrained and selective with their use of praise?

Gratitude

Expressing gratitude or appreciation is another gesture of considerable value in sports. In a world where the focus is so much on preparation and performance, expressing gratitude goes straight to the heart of a relationship between two people, not just between an athlete and a coach.

Some coaches start a meeting with simple routines like asking athletes to briefly say out loud what they appreciate about each other's contributions. Helping them do this more spontaneously is something you can keep an eye on and remind them about the value of. The experience of a team coming together to express gratitude to each other can be enormous for generating solidarity. When you know you are valued, you can really trust your teammates and play with the confidence that every coach values and hopes for.

Some athletes might not be that used to receiving gratitude. If you use it sensitively, it can be an excellent opportunity for young people to learn and grow through their involvement in sports. Table 5.2 highlights the different uses of affirmation, gratitude, and praise.

TABLE 5.2. Praise, Gratitude, and Affirmation: A Summary

Praise	Gratitude	Affirmation
"Well done; that was good stuff out there."	*"Thanks for helping with the setup for practice—much appreciated."*	*"You somehow found that extra gear out there."*
It's like alcohol. OK only in moderation. A little can lighten the mood, improve someone's day, or temporarily increase courage. Too much is toxic. It can create dysfunction and dependence, and can inhibit healthy habits.	It enhances relationship building and helps to bond a team but is not important for building athlete skill and motivation.	These are powerful skill-building boosters; inherently positive for the athlete.

Note. We thank Mary Hodorowicz for helping us with the summaries of praise, gratitude, and affirmation.

A "CAN-DO" ATTITUDE

The skill of affirming can light a fire inside athletes, even when things are not going well. It can also be part of a wider shift in coaching philosophy. Used in conversations with teammates, staff members, and coaches; in corridors and coffee rooms; and for more formal meetings, affirming can become a practical way of expressing respect for the talents of others, and for improving relationships all round. The team or club will be a better place to be in as a result.

When you affirm athletes, it can stick with them long after the effect of praise fades away, and it can affect well-being and performance for the better. The play in which they got it over the line will become a distant memory, but their recognition of their own courage can be a building block of confidence that they take into the next play and game. Using affirmation helps to steer the athlete's focus away from "can't-do" toward a more optimistic "can-do" attitude. They get to feel more capable, they sift through their talents and challenges, and they start to envision change. Here's how one very experienced elite coach, Michael Beale, put it when looking back on his own playing career: "When you're a good young player coming through, you tend to get a lot of pats on the back. But I needed more clarity from my coaches. . . . I couldn't articulate what I needed" (Beale, 2018). In using MI and skills like affirmation, you effectively help them to say what they need.

QUESTIONS TO CONSIDER

■ When was the last time someone expressed real gratitude to you for the work you are doing? What effect did this have on you?

■ When is punishment a good strategy with athletes?

■ Who was your favorite teacher or coach? How did he or she affirm you?

■ What are your two to three strongest qualities in your work in sports?

CHAPTER 6

Rolling with Athlete Resistance to Change

Force has no place where there is need of skill.
—HERODOTUS

HIGHLIGHTS

+ Confronting resistance can waste energy and backfire.
+ Rolling with resistance starts with calmness inside us.
+ Listening takes the energy out of resistance and rapidly decreases conflict so that athletes can take the next step.

THE KICKOFF

Your most important player had a tough game. He's a wreck in the locker room, head in hands, and he tells you straight, "I hope you understand it; I'm done with this team." That's resistance. You sense it first in your gut. Now what? Is your only choice to fight back, to counter force with force, with a reply like "Hang on a minute; that's unacceptable for a member of this team"? You'll get kickback for sure. Then what?

This was the kind of challenge that gave birth to MI, when a different stance to fighting force with force was unearthed. The idea was *not* to avoid facing tough issues but about calming things down to a point where they could be addressed constructively. The shift in strategy worked so well that the principle of "rolling with resistance"[1] formed an early foundation for MI. You use the core skills of MI (see Chapter 4) to help you overcome

[1]This phrase and the term "resistance" have since been replaced by a new framework; see Miller and Rollnick (2012).

68

these difficult situations. Then, once you have listened and things have calmed down, you can disagree with an athlete without being disagreeable, a skill that builds trust and leads to better decisions all around.

FROM THE FRONTLINE

Let's return to that locker room. It was an hour after a game that went all wrong. Toward the end of the final period, the players were arguing among themselves so much that a shouting match broke out on the field. Among them was a senior player who is usually calm, which is why the coach decided to have a word with him. He asks the player, "How come the team pressed the self-destruct button like that?" Little does the coach know what is coming.

> PLAYER: Easy for you to say! You weren't out there on the field. I was. I saw what was going on, and they were not trying. Their heads were down, and they were just lazy, so I cursed them out. That's it. I'll do it again. I'm done with this stupid team.
>
> (*Then the conversation continues, like a boxing match but with no winner. They are both standing up and in each other's face.*)
>
> COACH: Now hang on buddy, calm down; can't you take a bit of criticism?
>
> PLAYER: Can't you see what's going on for yourself? They are a bunch of losers.
>
> COACH: I think you should take a step back, OK?
>
> PLAYER: No, that's the problem. I'm the only one stepping up.
>
> COACH: Watch it! Calm down before you say something you'll regret.

By this point in your life, we assume you have learned that the least effective way to help someone calm down is to suggest that they calm down. Yet we still do it instinctively. Leaving that aside, if an athlete says something like "I'm done with this stupid team," it's quite strong resistance to what you might like to get across. How you reply can swing the conversation toward or away from resolution. Confronting resistance intensifies it. Indeed, how many clumsy exchanges like this might turn a corner and amount to bullying in sporting circles? How many coaches end up with broken relationships with athletes?

Confronting resistance intensifies it.

Rolling with resistance doesn't mean backing off, ignoring a problem, or just agreeing with an athlete but means coming alongside to calm things down *as a first step*; then you can address the problem itself. Here's an example:

> JAYSON: I'm doing my best coach! Why did you pull me out of the game like that? The goalie gets away with murder and then you pull me out for one little foul. [resistance]
>
> COACH: You're angry right now, and you think I'm being unfair. I get it. [listening statement]

JAYSON: One foul!

COACH: That doesn't seem fair to you. [affirming]

JAYSON: Yeah, you got it.

COACH: I want to hear more about how you can make good progress, but now isn't the right time for us to talk. We will; I promise you that. [rolling with resistance]

JAYSON: OK, Coach.

What Is Resistance?

To begin with, when we were developing MI, we found ourselves stumbling in conversations with clients who were emerging from the turmoil of broken personal and home lives—their language was strong, defiant, and full of denial or blaming others, a pattern that soon became evident in other settings such as law enforcement, health care, the military, and, indeed, sports as well. We then shifted our approach and tried not to argue people out of the position they had taken but rather to come alongside them and listen. The resistance we initially saw went down, and we realized these clients were not nearly as "unmotivated" as we had judged them to be. We had been merrily calling them "resistant" as if they had something deeply flawed inside them, using this and that label about them, laying the blame for a problem squarely on their shoulders, when in fact we had been "looking in the wrong place" for what might calm them down and motivate them to change. The problem lay to some extent in the way we had been speaking with them. It sent a shock wave through our work and led to the development of MI.

"Shift your style to a calmer, less confrontational one and things soon progress well" was the guideline we adopted. Does it work in everyday sporting exchanges? That's what we illustrate in this chapter. First up is your attitude.

An example that paints the picture of the MI-influenced exchange is the difference between the martial art of aikido and boxing. Aikido is a self-defense system developed in Japan. Its hallmark feature is that when applying this method, you rarely confront force with force. Instead, you exhaust your opponent by dodging and "rolling" with their aggressive energy. In some situations for self-defense, you have to transform their aggression into a counterattack. But boxing on the other hand is characterized by an all-out battle of wills—explosive force against explosive force. Even if someone wins, both participants end up bloody. When discussing things with resistant athletes, we try to allow for their force, even welcome it. The more we allow them room, within limits, to attack, the more we roll with it (just as aikido does), the more opportunity we have to avoid a damaging outcome and find a way through to a coachable moment.

Do You Recognize Resistance?

Here are some common and quite strong examples of resistance:

1. "I need to be in this game, Coach. My family is coming from out of town, and this is their only opportunity to watch me play."
2. "Why do you keep telling me to use my backhand for those balls? I can't hit it as hard with my backhand as my forehand. I need to get my best shot every time."
3. "I don't want to practice any more—I have to focus on my schoolwork. I can't play if I don't keep up my grades, and then what?"
4. "I have to discipline my horse when she is wrong. I can't just use praise—she'll never learn. I don't want to frustrate her."
5. "I keep trying to get my feet over my boots, but it makes me lean too far forward, and I'm afraid I'll fall. I think I'll get better faster if I just ski the way it feels right to me."

Notice how some forms of resistance reflect conflict or potential conflict between you and the athlete (number 1 and especially number 2), what we have called discord, while others reflect conflict within the athlete (numbers 3, 4, and 5).

Resistance is expressed not just in anger but also in all forms of reluctance and unwillingness. You will notice many of the behaviors listed in Box 6.1, all indications of resistance.

It's About Your Relationship

When athletes say these kinds of things, it's tempting to wonder who is to blame and get sucked into confronting the problem; however, our starting point is perhaps a simpler one: The connection between you is not solid, it's a relationship problem, and you can repair the damage. How? By not meeting force with force—instead use "aikido style." Connect by using a following style, and resistance will go down. Then you can be honest and open and begin to tackle the problem.

A Different Approach When Things Go Wrong

It's easy enough to wield authority and use a fixing style to confront and stamp out problems, even punish athletes. Rolling with resistance is not

---

BOX 6.1. Signals of Resistance

Reluctance: "I'm not sure I play that way, Coach."
Challenging: "That's not true. I was in position like you asked me to be."
Minimizing: "My diet isn't as bad as you say."
Hostility: "I don't like the way you order me around like that on the court."
Talking over: Athlete talks over you, effectively unwilling to listen.
Unwillingness to change: "No, I don't want to play that position."
Cutting off: "Now wait a minute. I'm saying it was my best game."
Inattention: It's clear that the athlete, absorbed in a smartphone, has not been following what you say.
Blaming: "This is not my fault we lost; it's hers."
Sidetracking: The athlete client changes the direction of the conversation.
Disagreeing: "Yes, but I don't think your strategy will work."
Nonanswer: In answering a query, the athlete gives a response that is not an answer to the question.
Excusing: "How am I supposed to know they were going to change the play?"

Adapted from Miller and Rollnick (1992).

---

just a strategy but a signal you send out about a different approach, where you help athletes to learn from mistakes and conflicts by helping them to say how and why they might improve. That's MI in a nutshell. It's based on caring about the person you are talking to.

MINDSET AND SKILLS

Stepping Back, Staying Loose, and Rolling with It

When athletes say things that sound angry, reluctant, disengaged, or distracted, it can be difficult not to tighten up and leap in with your solutions or counterargument, let alone do as we suggest and *accept* that they feel the

> Accepting the person doesn't mean agreeing about the problem.

way they do, even if you strongly disagree. Yet the mindset requirement for rolling with resistance is precisely that. Here's one way of looking at it: There's a person and there's a problem; accepting the person is not the same as agreeing about the problem. There's a time for listening and a time for stepping in to address the problem. When resistance is strong, you will find that it's better to listen than to counter it. Once you have earned respect by listening, and the connection between you and the athlete is better, you can use the calmer atmosphere to address the main problem. You'll find the athlete much more motivated than you might have initially believed.

Once you decide to stay calm, loosen up, and let go of judgment about the athlete's attitude and motivation, what next? The rest of this chapter will address this challenge. If possible, go somewhere a little quieter and sit down with the athlete. Then what?

FROM THE FRONTLINE

There's a saying that's used with coaches that goes like this: "Stay on your side of the net!" As sports become more and more international, there are increasing cultural misunderstandings with coaches and players coming from different countries. One common observation is that coaches from the United States and Europe show respect by looking into a player's eyes when speaking about an important topic. But players from some Asian and Latin American countries are raised to avert eye contact. Many coaches make assumptions about this lack of eye contact. They assume a certain level of disrespect or lack of motivation or resistance when they witness this behavior. One concept that is helpful in this situation or others in which we share a cultural background is to work on avoiding assumptions about why a player is doing something that bothers us. In other words, "stay on your side of the net" and try not to assign a motive to an athlete's resistant behavior. There's another saying attributed to the football coach Urban Meyer: "Stay curious, not furious." This captures well an MI stance when presented with resistance, be it a cultural misunderstanding or something else.

Ask a Few Genuinely Curious Questions

Rolling with resistance is the opposite of what they call "upping the ante." Questions like these will get you started: "Let's step back a moment. How do you really see it?" or "What exactly went on for you?" If you allow athletes to talk, they will calm down as their story unfolds. Apologize about a misunderstanding, if necessary, knowing that humility is a virtue (and sometimes requires practice).

Use Listening Statements

Listening statements really come into their own in the face of resistance, especially after you have asked a nonconfrontational open question. It's a bit like being alongside the athlete on a squash court, rackets and ball in hand, with the wall in front of you. Your task is to hit the ball so that it's as easy as possible for the athlete to return it. That's how it feels when making listening statements in the face of resistance.

EXERCISE 6.1. What makes it better or worse?

Consider the following exchanges. Make a decision for yourself about which reply makes things better and which make them worse.

> ATHLETE: I'm not sure I can keep going here. I'm not carrying on with all this. I'm just fed up. Coach, I've tried my best, but I'm just not cut out for this I guess. [resistance]
>
> REPLY 1: So you can't really take the pressure here anymore.
>
> REPLY 2: It's getting you down.
>
> REPLY 3: What's going on then?

Which reply is a listening statement designed to "lower the temperature," so to speak, and understand the athlete's position? Reply 1, probably said with an air of sarcasm, will make things worse. Reply 3 is a question not a statement; it's probably useful but not the skill we are focused on here, which is the listening statement. Reply 2 hits the mark well, is a statement, and won't make things worse. It captures fairly accurately what the athlete has said. She will feel understood and will carry on telling you how she feels, calming down as she does so. An unwinding process as you roll with her resistance could look like this:

> ATHLETE: Coach, I've tried my best, but I'm just not cut out for this I guess. [resistance]
>
> COACH: It's getting you down. [listening statement]
>
> ATHLETE: Yes, I'm sick of all the yelling and screaming around here and the way we always get blamed for any defeat.
>
> COACH: It's not helpful. [listening statement]
>
> ATHLETE: You can say that again. I mean, why can't people be more calm and supportive around here.
>
> COACH: People chilling out a bit would help you. [listening statement]
>
> ATHLETE: It would for sure, but fat chance that will happen, and that's why I'm sick of it.
>
> COACH: I wonder what I might do to help? [open question]
>
> ATHLETE: I mean, it's great to just get some of this off my chest. What would you do if you were me? (*much calmer now*)

EXERCISE 6.2. A parent is angry with you.

> PARENT: This is not fair; you haven't picked my son for the game in three weeks. [resistance]
>
> REPLY 1: Well, I have a whole team to think about.
>
> REPLY 2: Please come and see me before practice next week, OK?
>
> REPLY 3: You want to do the best by your son in this sport.

Reply 3 provides the best example of using a listening statement to address this parent's concern. Its use doesn't mean you agree or disagree, simply that you are stepping back and coming alongside. The parent will start to calm down. Reply 1 is going to up the ante and generate kickback. Reply 2 will leave the parent seething with frustration.

EXERCISE 6.3. A player is reluctant to change position.

COACH: I've made the decision to change your position, OK?

ATHLETE: You can do what you want. You're the coach. [resistance]

REPLY 1: This feels unfair to you.

REPLY 2: I don't do this without careful thought, my friend.

REPLY 3: You want me to always give you what you want.

This example is hard because the athlete is angry with the coach. It's often more difficult to stay calm when you are the object of anger.

Which reply will have the athlete feeling best understood? It's clearly the first one. The second one is an example of not rolling with resistance but returning fire with fire. The third is way off the mark, like a ball that is poorly played and lands somewhere unexpected and unhelpful, difficult for the athlete to respond to.

Put a little bluntly, rolling with resistance involves taking a moment to step back and reflect before opening your mouth. This requires the hard work of practicing the MI mindset described in Chapter 2. Just because you know you want to listen doesn't mean you will be able to when the pressure is on and an athlete's emotion is running high. Practicing the skills outlined in Chapter 4 will help you stay cool as you get better at rolling with resistance.

CONFLICT INSIDE THE ATHLETE

Most of the above examples are of resistance directed at you. However, you can also come face-to-face with resistance that's got nothing to do with you or conflict in the relationship that is an expression of conflict inside the athlete. Who doesn't feel ambivalent sometimes (see Chapter 3)? You might have simply asked, "How are you doing?" and you get a reply like these below:

"It's just not working out, this new routine."

or

"I don't really want to change positions."

or

"I can't keep coming to practice."

These statements are often only one voice in athletes' minds, but there are others, often in opposition and in positive contrast to what they have just said. This player could have responded just as sincerely with two of those voices. For example:

> "It's just not working out this new routine, *yet I'd like to make it work well.*"
>
> *or*
>
> "I don't really want to change positions, *but maybe I should try.*"
>
> *or*
>
> "I can't keep coming to practice, *but I do like this sport and the people in the club.*"

That's what we mean by "jail cell of doubt" (see Chapter 3, p. 34), a normal conflict in which, as they try to move forward, athletes feel trapped by opposing motivations. One voice in their mind says one thing; another says the opposite.

Under these circumstances, to argue against the negative, or try to persuade the athlete "out of" the problem, produces exactly what you might not want to hear. You will fall into that "Yes, but . . ." trap we mentioned in Chapter 1.

> ATHLETE: I don't really want to change positions.
>
> COACH: Can't you see that in the long run this will be better for you?
>
> ATHLETE: Yes, but today I will struggle, and next thing I'll get dropped from the team.
>
> COACH: Your position today will be best for the team as well, and I need to think about that too.
>
> ATHLETE: Sure, but why sacrifice me? I'm doing fine in my normal position.

As you list the advantages, he hears himself talk about the disadvantages. You want to avoid falling into what we have called the persuasion trap. Instead, if you come alongside and listen, he will calm down, and soon you can ask him about the positive side. It can take just a minute or two to help athletes come unstuck, a lot longer if you leave them seething in the jail cell of doubt or ambivalence.

MOVING BEYOND RESISTANCE

Here's how that short conversation with the athlete who is reluctant to change positions might look if you roll with his initial disappointment.

You'll see how MI fits in toward the end, where the coach helps him to talk about the advantages of a change in field position. The athlete hears himself present the case for change, his motivation lifts, and their relationship is strengthened immeasurably as a result.

> ATHLETE: There's no way I should be playing wing.
>
> COACH: It seems to you it's not the best place for you to have an impact. [listening statement]
>
> ATHLETE: Not really. Well, I'd like to think I can be useful in a number of positions [change talk], but this is not my favorite.
>
> COACH: Right—it's not your favorite, but you pride yourself on being a versatile player. [listening statement]
>
> ATHLETE: I guess so, but I also need to feel there's an option to go back on defense so I don't lose my place; it's always been *my* position.
>
> COACH: So, as long as you are performing well, and that is recognized, you are more open to a move. [listening statement, a guess]
>
> ATHLETE: It's not so much the change in position; it's more being moved out so the new guy can fit into the team.
>
> COACH: It's tough being asked to do something different than you are used to. [affirmation]
>
> ATHLETE: Yep, but I know I have to perform well wherever I play.

Rolling with resistance is not the same as agreeing with what athletes are saying or "letting them off the hook." Think of it like this: if there were a fire, what would you do? You wouldn't waste energy on whose fault it is (blaming) or run around saying it's not your responsibility to put it out. You wouldn't pour gasoline on it or say, "Well, it's only in the kitchen not anywhere else." You'd put it out.[2]

WATCHFUL AND SKILLFUL

As athletes learn to anticipate better in competition, their performance will improve. This observation applies here too in your conversations with athletes: Anticipating how a player will respond when resistance is high is the first step in improving your performance as a coach for lifting motivation. Rolling with resistance is a skill, and it's also an attitude, of wanting to help and coming alongside an athlete to improve your connection. Instead

---

[2] Thanks to Mary Hodorowicz for telling us about this analogy.

of falling into a hole athletes are in and making it deeper, we join up with them, step out of it with them together, and see a better way ahead.

QUESTIONS TO CONSIDER

- What do you do when you start to feel angry with an athlete?
- When athletes get angry, how do you react? What does this trigger in you?
- Under what conditions is it good to express anger with athletes and teams?
- Why might young athletes lie to you and not to their friends?

PART II

TOOLBOX

The former Olympic athlete and now journalist Matthew Syed gave himself the task of trying to understand how a lowly placed soccer team, Leicester City, managed in the space of one season to rise to the top of the toughest league in the world—the English Premier League. He must have been speaking from personal experience when he remarked:

> For many decades, sport . . . has operated with a basic model of coaching and motivation. If you were being diplomatic, you would call it the didactic approach. If you were being a little more honest, you would call it dictatorship. The idea was that motivation was achieved by fear. Players were essentially uneducated and idle, and the only way they could be brought into line was through cracking the whip. Tactics and instructions were handed down from on high. The players were like manual labourers, expected to listen and obey. (Syed, 2016)

For Syed, something different happened in that magical year for Leicester City in 2016, and from inside accounts it emerged that when the newly appointed coach looked back, he regarded the fact that he listened to players in a key early meeting as the defining moment that changed everything.

If the behavior of parents and coaches on the side of youth sports playing fields is anything to go by, Syed's observation of a top-down approach to coaching is not confined to elite sports. Parents who feel genuinely passionate about wanting their children to do well can end up yelling and screaming at wide-eyed and fearful young people. In truth, what children and young people enjoy the most about sports are fun, friendship, and freedom of expression, not winning at all costs.

How can athletes of all ages be listened to, supported, and freed up to express themselves and learn new skills? MI provides a toolbox that contains skills such as asking and listening that we have worked on in different scenarios. With experience came a set of strategies where the skills could be combined to address different sporting challenges, and that's what we present here in Part II. You will find strategies for connecting with players (Chapter 7), addressing motivation and behavior problems (Chapter 8), setting goals (Chapter 9), and giving advice and feedback (Chapter 10). This list of chapters allows you to select a topic of greatest interest and see where and how you can use MI on and around the field of competition.

Connecting Rapidly

Everybody can communicate, but are they connected?
—PAUL MCGUINNESS, soccer coach

HIGHLIGHTS

+ Choose your moment
+ *Strategies:* (1) Declutter your mind, and stay present;
  (2) Listen, and reflect on what you hear and, if necessary,
  summarize.
+ Remember he or she is a person, not just an athlete, and
  highlight the person's strengths as you go along.
+ Connect afresh each time because the athlete's situation is
  never static.

Before stepping in with advice or solutions, you can start most conversations with athletes by connecting with them. Doing this rapidly doesn't mean rushing—it's a skill set involving at its heart listening (Chapter 4). It's one thing to be approachable and keen to connect but something else when you have the skills to back this up.

THE KICKOFF

"Connecting well" is widely talked about in sports, yet is not viewed as a skill with which the more you practice, the more efficient, simple, and effective its use becomes. As we all know, sports attracts high emotion like a lightning rod, where it's so easy to misunderstand each other, fall out, withdraw into unhappy states, form cliques, or feel rejected. Yet it is possible to connect routinely so that setbacks become more manageable and athletes are set free to enjoy their sport and focus on what really matters.

The diversity of scenarios calling for rapid connecting is almost endless, and this might include connecting with fellow coaches, staff members, the family of players, and even media.

FROM THE FRONTLINE

He was an international athlete but was regularly second to his archrival. Unbeknownst to his support team, he kept a diary about his progress in competition. One day his coach noticed him writing a note after a practice session.

This was an opportunity to connect, which happened rapidly not only because the coach listened but because of what he held back from doing (rushing, advising, interrupting, changing the subject, or raising or solving a problem). Notice how you can even start a conversation with a listening statement, an observation, not a question.

COACH: Wow, that's a lot of notes you seem to writing. [listening statement]

ATHLETE: Oh, I never meant you to see them.

COACH: Oh, sorry. I hope you don't mind too much; you are clearly working hard on all this.

ATHLETE: Yeah, it's OK if you see them (*blushing*); it's kinda obsessive, but I like to review what works and what doesn't [change talk].

COACH: You want to bring a sharp eye to your progress. [listening statement and affirmation]

ATHLETE: Yeah, it helps, but it's also disappointing when I don't do well enough.

COACH: Yet these notes tell you things that could be helpful. [listening statement]

ATHLETE: Yeah, exactly, win or lose, I try to learn from them [change talk].

COACH: So, this has been your special diary, and win or lose you want to make it work for you. [listening statement]

ATHLETE: Yes, that's exactly how I feel about them.

COACH: There is something deep inside you that pushes you to master yourself. [listening statement and affirmation]

ATHLETE: I'm not sure about that! But maybe—yeah, I do feel determined to find my best [change talk].

COACH: Maybe we can look at the notes together and see what will help?

ATHLETE: I'm relieved you have seen them now, so the secret is out. (*Laughs.*) Yes, please, let's see how they can help.

The connection they established was simple, profound, and a turning point. A new training strategy emerged, and at the next international event he wasn't second! When the coach made every effort just to connect and understand, their relationship reached a new level of trust and safety for the athlete, who moved from a secret note-taker to working on things with his coach to remarkably good effect.

> Connecting happens rapidly when you don't interrupt, change the subject, or solve a problem.

What about these three scenarios—how might you connect here?

1. You are meeting an athlete for the first time.
2. She's upset, on a "bad run," and her performance is just not there.
3. You need to tell him he's dropped for the next game, and he won't like it.

STRATEGY: DECLUTTER YOUR MIND AND STAY PRESENT

Summary: Make the decision to *only* connect and not to achieve anything else. You plan to connect by listening. Take a deep breath or two, and approach with a curious attitude.

Connecting can be mistaken for being friendly. For sure, this is a good starting point, to be approachable, with your "green light" on, open to whatever conversation comes your way. You might deliberately take a walk through the locker room to ready yourself and be available, ready to take an interest not just in the athletes but also in their lives away from sports. That kind of willingness can go a long way. And then there's something else: the *ability* to listen. This is where connecting becomes very practical, even technical.

> **TIP:** *Choose your moment to connect, and put nothing in the way of listening.*

Imagine trying to listen to two or more people at the same time. That's what a cluttered mind feels like. All too often we are thinking simultaneously about how to coach, strategic alignments, planning for practice, and the next competition. We often listen to "reply" rather than to "understand." When approaching a player, our need to help them adds to all this clutter and gets in the way of listening. The starting point for rapid connecting is a mind free of clutter and distraction. Box 7.1 contains a list of distractions, barriers to connecting rapidly.

BOX 7.1. Barriers to Connecting

- *Prematurely searching for solutions.* The mother of all roadblocks: You search for solutions before you have even connected with the athlete.
- *Rushing.* Having other things on your mind and feeling under time pressure will be noticed by athletes. Connection will suffer accordingly.
- *Changing the subject or interrupting.* A most unfortunate and common mistake. Try not to block the flow and "stay in the groove" until you have a shared grasp of the athlete's experience.
- *Confronting, arguing, or passing judgment.* This is like erecting a large barrier, for example, if you start to blame or label the athlete as a problem to be solved. You can expect fairly immediate shutdown.
- *Needing to be in control.* How much of a challenge might this be for you? While you listen, you hand control over to the athlete for a while.

TIP: *Try not to solve a problem, change the subject, rush, argue, pass judgment, or take control of the conversation.*

Connecting is not about intervening or trying to get *your* message across but about understanding the athlete. Your jumping in with an agenda will work against what needs to occur. If you approach the athlete skillfully, the connecting will happen quickly because of the things you *don't* do. "Less is more" in these conversations.

TIP: *Take a few deep breaths before you start connecting. A lot of our ability to stay present is governed by our mental state. Taking a few slow breaths in through you nose and out through your mouth can center you and improve your readiness to observe and connect with an athlete or the team as a whole.*

To listen well you want to be in the present moment, focused on the other person. A simple breathing exercise before you get going can help enormously. With distractions to one side, it can feel as if time is standing still, as if you have more time on your hands than you thought you had. Your mind will feel clearer, which allows you to focus on listening. A psychologist we know described this as coming to a "full stop." We've all been in a vehicle, a car, or boat in which we are coasting along slowly. When we truly listen, we come to a full stop. This means we put on our mental brakes and focus all our attention on the person

Jumping in with an agenda works against connecting.

in front of us. We aren't rolling along, winging it by being halfway present. We are putting down everything in our hands and on our minds to truly sit with the athlete in front of us and take in this person's point of view.

The Strategy in Action

She's a hard-working athlete who also takes a caring role with her siblings. She comes through the door looking very stressed.

> COACH: Hi, Cindy. You look rushed.
>
> ATHLETE: You can say that again . . . kids to school, traffic; there's times I don't feel I can do this much longer.
>
> COACH: It's that balancing act again.
>
> ATHLETE: Yeah, exactly. I try, really I do, and then there's always something that gets in the way.
>
> COACH: And you managed to get here today.
>
> ATHLETE: Yeah, thanks; you got me. I want to keep going here if I can. I'll catch up with you later, and thanks for checking in with me like that.

Replay the Tape

Statement	What's going on?
COACH: Hi, Cindy. You look rushed.	*Listening statement. Feeling no need even for a greeting, the coach simply focused on what Cindy might be experiencing. It was a guess, an invitation for her to confirm, reject, or elaborate, like handing a baton over to her. It's direct and time efficient.*
ATHLETE: You can say that again . . . kids to school, traffic; there's times I don't feel I can do this much longer.	*She says a lot in a few words, including a suggestion that she could quit the sport. The coach might be tempted to step in and address this (e.g., "Oh, no, don't give up; we love having you around here"). However, the logic behind rapid connecting is to not "take the bait" and to focus on listening instead.*

Statement	What's going on?
COACH: It's that balancing act again.	*Listening statement. The coach tries again to capture what she is experiencing, in as few words as possible, leaving it to Cindy to expand as she sees fit.*
ATHLETE: Yeah, exactly. I try, really I do, and then there's always something that gets in the way.	*She confirms the accuracy of the coach's guess about the balancing act.*
COACH: And you managed to get here today.	*Uses affirmation to highlight strengths.*
ATHLETE: Yeah, thanks; you got me. I want to keep going here if I can. I'll catch up with you later, and thanks for checking in with me like that.	*Cindy confirms the accuracy of the coach's guesses and responds with change talk ("I want to keep going here if I can").*

Conclusion

The coach was fully present and free of distraction when she made that opening statement to Cindy. It then took just a minute of thoughtful listening for Cindy to say, "Yeah, thanks; you got me." That's rapid connecting. When the coach stepped away from a problem-solving state of mind and chose to listen instead, the coach took the pressure out of the situation and Cindy found the motivation inside herself to say, "I want to keep going here if I can." The effect of listening was to convey an empowering message to her: "I believe in you, your strengths, and your own good judgment." The outcome was that her motivation shifted in a positive direction.

> **TIP:** *Remember, this is a person, not just an athlete, and someone with strengths too. Wearing "strengths lenses," highlighted in Chapter 2 (p. 23), will bring immediate rewards.*

Being 100% present isn't easy, but it is a mental task that can be practiced. Each time you work toward coming to a "full stop" in a conversation, even in increments of 60 seconds, you will increase your ability to connect. Over time, as your skillfulness in listening improves, it will become an easier groove to slip into ("OK, now I am in listening mode").

It requires work to resist the righting reflex in these situations. We feel the need to correct and advise. By focusing on connecting there, we don't give up the opportunity to guide and potentially fix later; we simply make the later effort to do so likely more effective.

STRATEGY: LISTEN AND REFLECT WHAT YOU HEAR

Summary: You might start with an open question, but try to follow this with listening statements, affirmation, and, if necessary, a summary.

When connecting, the idea is not to get in the way of athletes saying how they are feeling. Your job is to simply wonder, *What's* really *going on for this person?* You ask questions and also reflect what you hear and understand by using listening statements.

> **TIP:** *Ask open questions, but try not to rely on them—using listening statements will ensure better progress.*

Check Chapter 3 to remind you of the techniques involved in making listening statements. If you are genuinely curious, these often come out quite naturally. You capture the essence in your own mind about what athletes might be feeling and then hand this over to them in a statement, a guess, or a hypothesis.

Imagine playing the game of squash where the aim is to make it as easy as possible for your partner to play a good shot in return. That's what you aim to do with listening statements, so that the athlete makes the best possible progress.

> It's like volleying soft shots your tennis partner can easily return.

The Strategy in Action

Carlos is about to head out into a game, and when you greet him, he looks really down, disconnected from you and all else. You sense immediately that being bright and friendly is not going to lift the mood, and however tempting it might be to urge him to brighten up or even suggest a way of doing this, can you just connect with him and then consider what to do next?

COACH: Hi, Carlos. Can I have a word before you head out there?

CARLOS: Yeah.

COACH: How are you doing?

CARLOS: Hey, not good, and I've got a game to play.

COACH: You're not feeling right.

CARLOS: Too much shit at home.

COACH: Things are not going so well.

CARLOS: No, we got family problems at home.

COACH: And now you have to get focused on this game coming up.

CARLOS: Exactly, Coach, but I'm gonna try; I promise you that.

COACH: When would be a good time for us to talk more about this?

CARLOS: I'm fine now. I'll maybe catch you afterward.

(Then later on . . .)

COACH: Seemed like you worked really hard out there.

CARLOS: Yes, my mind was on the game, but I'm not relaxed at all. I'm working hard not to let it get in the way.

COACH: It's not easy balancing life and sports.

CARLOS: I just hope things can calm down and give me a break to get myself back in a good zone.

COACH: Let me know if you want to catch up tomorrow, or anytime. I'm here to help you in whatever way I can.

CARLOS: Hey, thanks.

Replay the Tape

Statement	What's going on?
COACH: Hi, Carlos. Can I have a word before you head out there?	*The tougher the situation, the wiser it is to ask permission and give him a choice about what he wants to say.*
CARLOS: Yeah.	
COACH: How are you doing?	*Simple open question. Now the coach needs to be ready to listen.*
CARLOS: Hey, not good, and I've got a game to play.	
COACH: You're not feeling right.	*Listening statement. It's easy to start a guessing game now by asking lots of questions, such as "Have you got struggles in college?" Instead, the simplest of listening statements gives Carlos the freedom to say what's up, if he wants to. It's more efficient too.*
CARLOS: Too much shit at home.	*That's a very open-hearted reply.*
COACH: Things are not going so well.	*Listening statement. Again, the coach imagines his experience and offers*

Statement	What's going on?
	a cautious guess in the form of a listening statement.
CARLOS: No, we got family problems at home.	*Carlos notices the genuine interest and is therefore happy to reveal more.*
COACH: And now you have to get focused on this game coming up.	*Listening statement. Coach wonders whether Carlos is reluctant to talk more because he is about to play in a match. So he forms a listening statement using that idea. Is he right?*
CARLOS: Exactly, Coach, but I'm gonna try; I promise you that.	*Carlos confirms his readiness to head out into the game as best he can (that's change talk).*
COACH: When would be a good time for us to talk more about this?	*Checks whether Carlos wants to talk more.*
CARLOS: I'm fine now. I'll maybe catch you afterward.	
(*Then later on . . .*)	
COACH: Seemed like you worked really hard out there.	*He opens the conversation with a listening statement that was an affirmation (not praise; see Chapter 5).*
CARLOS: Yes, my mind was on the game, but I'm not relaxed at all. I'm working hard not to let it get in the way.	*Carlos is more than ready to engage. Notice the change talk ("I'm working hard not to let it get in the way").*
COACH: It's not easy balancing life and sports.	*A listening statement that captures the essence of his dilemma.*
CARLOS: I just hope things can calm down and give me a break to get myself back in a good zone.	*The response is a form of change talk.*
COACH: Let me know if you want to catch up tomorrow, or anytime. I'm here to help you in whatever way I can.	*He winds up leaving the door open to further conversation another time.*
CARLOS: Hey, thanks.	

Conclusion

Two brief conversations of rapid connecting with Carlos established a firm foundation for their relationship and for addressing problems at home when the time is right. Because the coach ensured that those mental distractions were absent or under control, he had the time and space to capture in his own mind what Carlos was feeling and hand this over to him in a listening statement.

If the conversation is a little longer than those above, consider the value of a summary that pulls together what athletes have said, with a special emphasis on their strengths and aspirations. With Carlos, for example, after discussing problems at home, the coach might summarize thus: "Tell me if I have understood you right, Carlos: You want things to change at home because the stress there is holding you back big time. You are tired of seeing your mother spoken to rudely by your sister and behaving like she does, and you might even ask her to go and live somewhere else. What you want is to focus on your sport right now. Have I left anything out?"

Each day is a fresh day when it comes to connecting. Just because an athlete felt one thing on one day holds no certainty for how he or she feels the next day. Similarly, even if you feel you have a good relationship in general, a new day or a new session carries the likelihood of added value in reconnecting. The better you know an athlete, the less time this will probably take.

TIP: *Connect afresh each time because their situation is never static.*

RAPID CONNECTING IN THE BROADER ORGANIZATION

The word *relationships* is often championed as an expression of team or club culture, even mounted on walls to remind everyone of the value of the human side of sporting life. Does rapid connecting provide a practical way of improving organizational relationships?

Imagine a scenario in which you are not alone in your ability to connect with players, but you work with colleagues who have this ability as well. Like the lighting of small fires, the more connecting that takes place in a club, the better the atmosphere and the better able athletes will be to solve problems and reach their potential within and outside of competition. Rapid connecting can provide the fuel that drives organizational change toward a truly collegial and supportive culture.

Sport is graced by countless daily demonstrations of caring, of a willingness to listen and be helpful. The grander and heartwarming gestures that hit the headlines only serve to reinforce what is known in every corner of sports: To succeed, an athlete will place considerable value on teammates and coaches with whom he or she can share concerns or aspirations, knowing that the respect and trust will endure regardless of the problem being discussed. Progress will be quicker when an athlete feels safe to broach whatever is bothering her or him. Connecting is the first step and is often enough in itself.

> Connecting is the first step and is often enough in itself.

QUESTIONS TO CONSIDER

- When you address problems with athletes, how often do you listen and connect first?
- How could being too friendly with athletes interfere with your effectiveness as a coach?
- How might you ask athletes what they need?
- Do you talk fast? If so, how might this interfere when you want an athlete to reflect about some issue? Can you slow down when it's needed?

CHAPTER 8

Lifting Motivation
THREE STRATEGIES

And then ultimately what I tell the kids is: coaches can give you
information, they can give you guidelines, and they can put you in a
position. But the only person who can truly make you better is you.
—BRANDI CHASTAIN, soccer coach

HIGHLIGHTS

+ Do athletes have the answer inside them to adapt their
  behavior or approach? Ask them. Assume they have the
  resources to make the changes.
+ Avoid making judgments about motivation—rather ask the
  athlete. Motivation is seldom black or white, and its strength
  changes regularly.
+ *Strategies:* (1) follow, guide, and then fix; (2) assess
  motivation; and (3) the "why" and "how" of change.
+ Establish a good connection, and look for solutions together.
  Avoid leaping in with a fixing style.

With a curious mindset, the flexible use of communication styles, and
the skills of MI, it is possible to draw out of athletes the motivation and
ideas for improvement, even in the face of difficult behavior.

THE KICKOFF

There's a saying, apparently from an African country, that goes like this:
"Go alone, go faster; go together, go farther." It's relevant here, now: If you
see an athlete's motivation flagging or held back by doubt, it's easy enough

to bang away at the problem at great speed, making little progress, but how do you approach this together, and make better progress? We kicked off this book in Chapter 1 with this challenge, and now we get right into the heart of the matter—using the mindset and skills of MI to make a difference in everyday conversations.

When we see an athlete struggling to get to the next level, we're likely left really wanting to help. It can also swing the other way, such as when we feel irritated or even angry because we think an athlete is disconnected or not focusing clearly enough. Either way, motivation raises its head, and there's a question about how to improve matters.

FROM THE FRONTLINE

His record on paper reads like a dream: a young man with such talent and flair who rose up to college-level competition through the age groups despite all the odds back home. Now he saunters in late for practice and aggravates you because he behaves as if his sport owes him a big favor. Some of his teammates look up to him, and others feel he doesn't want to be part of the group. If the team loses, he blames everyone else but himself. You have tried to encourage him to arrive in good time for practice. You have also talked with him about his goals for the season. What can you do or say that will make a difference?

STRATEGY: FOLLOW, GUIDE, AND THEN FIX

Summary: Instead of confronting a problem like that by only using a fixing style, consider the following sequence of styles: follow first, then guide, and if necessary, fix. Athletes are then more likely to take an active role in motivating themselves to change their behavior.

It can drain you of energy when you feel that someone's attitude or behavior *ought* to change. You have your goals, athletes have theirs, and how do you connect? You might even feel like screaming out, "How many times must I tell you to . . . ?"

"OK, can you just try this one more time?" [Athlete looks blank.]
"Well, now I wonder. Your times have dropped. Maybe you should party less and sleep more."
"It's a team game, and you are letting us all down. I want you to be on time for practice, and you never seem to get it right."
"Your academics are just as important as your sport, my friend, and now you could be heading for trouble, because your grades are nose-diving. You can't play if you aren't at this school anymore!"
"I ask you once, I ask you twice, and you still stray out of position."

Now what? How do you lift their motivation and desire to do better? It's not always so easy. Here's an example of hitting your head against a brick wall:

COACH: I want to have a word with you about showing up late for practice. It's not the first time, and I want to be straight with you: You need to make the effort to be on time.

ATHLETE: Oh, but it's just that by the time I get up and cross town, it always seems to be a little bit late. [resistance]

COACH: Listen, just get up a little earlier. Don't just do it for me . . . do it for the team. It will make a big difference. [Fixing style]

ATHLETE: Yeah, OK, man, but I don't think it's too big a deal, as you know when I am here I play just as well as the rest of them.

COACH: Well, I need to be clear with you; if this happens again, I might have to drop you from the team for a while.

ATHLETE: Hey, chill out, please, Coach. I do my best around here any-way.

COACH: OK, but be warned that the next time this happens. . . .

ATHLETE: Fine. Whatever you say, Coach, but it doesn't happen every day.

Notice the "yes, but"? Think of these as offsides in sports. Things are going fine; then the motivation momentum stops. This stoppage shows up in things like defensiveness, minimizing, arguing back, or shoulder shrug-ging. And the most frustrating part of this? It's we, not the players, who are offsides. It's wasted time and effort. The good news? We can fix it by using the "Follow, Guide, and then Fix" approach.

MI was developed for just this kind of challenge, where you want to avoid a fruitless battle of wills so you don't lose your enduring connection with the athlete. Can you avoid feeling cornered into either being a "play-ers' coach," that is, "soft" on unhelpful behavior, or a "disciplinarian," constantly correcting things and calling players out? How can you find a way of being that is "hard on the problem but

_____

Avoid a battle of wills. soft on the person"? What we call the "follow,
_____   guide, and then fix" strategy enables you to do

just this. You don't need to fall into the trap of hitting your head against a brick wall or resorting to blaming and punishment.

If you go back to Chapter 2 where we presented three possible styles—fixing, guiding, and following—you'll see that this coach's first and only strategy was to use a fixing style. It's a pity because a style that works so well in setting up practice routines and so many other things falls short here, and two decent people descend into a bit of a winner-takes-all exchange. What about the impact? Is it possible that the exclusive reliance on a fixing style has made him *less* likely to commit to changing? That was the starting point in the development of MI, and the reason we developed the strategy below.

The Strategy in Action: A New Lineup— Follow, Guide, and Then Fix

When you feel that itch telling you that trouble is brewing, instead of jumping in with a fixing style, how would it look if you use a sequence like this: follow, guide, and *then* fix (see Figure 8.1)?

Following Style, Briefly Used to Connect (1 Minute)

COACH: I want to have a word with you about showing up late for practice.

ATHLETE: Oh, sorry, Coach, but it's just that by the time I get up and cross town, it always seems to be a little bit late.

COACH: I appreciate your apology.

ATHLETE: Hey, no big deal. I always try my best when I'm here.

COACH: Even though you get here late, you are still committed to the club.

ATHLETE: Oh, for sure, man. As I say, I am sorry it happens like this.

COACH: It's not so easy for you to always get here on time.

ATHLETE: Exactly. I try to do most things right, but this is one thing that's not perfect.

Switch to a Guiding Style to Bring Out His Ideas about Change

COACH: Can I ask you, what might you do to get here on time?

ATHLETE: I'm not sure . . .

COACH: It could be hard for you to find a way.

Follow ⟶ Guide ⟶ Fix

FIGURE 8.1. Follow, guide, and then fix.

ATHLETE: I don't see it as such a big deal, to be honest, but yes, maybe I just go to bed too late and then it catches up with me in the morning.

COACH: You can see what might need to change.

ATHLETE: Not sure, man, but I'll try going to bed earlier.

End with a Fixing Style

COACH: I wanted to let you in on my thinking on why I've raised this with you today. We had to delay our strategy discussion until you arrived. We can't function well as a unit until everyone comes to practice on time.

ATHLETE: Sure, I get it, Coach.

COACH: Sometimes I'm forced to use sanctions like dropping people from the team, and this is the last thing I want to do with you.

ATHLETE: Sure, thanks for saying that because I'm here to start every game. I'll do my best, Coach.

Replay the Tape

Statement	What's going on?
COACH: I want to have a word with you about showing up late for practice.	*Coach looks for the right moment and takes a deep breath to get into the right mindset before asking permission to talk about a problem. Uses only a <u>following</u> style to begin with.*
ATHLETE: Oh, sorry, Coach, but it's just that by the time I get up and cross town, it always seems to be a little bit late.	*Initially open and apologetic, then defensive.*
COACH: I appreciate your apology.	
ATHLETE: Hey, no big deal. I always try my best when I'm here.	*Change talk.*
COACH: Even though you get here late, you are still committed to the club.	*Listening statement, captures both sides of a dilemma, and ends with the positive side (change talk).*

Statement	What's going on?
ATHLETE: Oh, for sure, man. As I say, I am sorry it happens like this.	*Athlete lowers defenses, and they begin to connect.*
COACH: It's not so easy for you to always get here on time.	*Listening statement.*
ATHLETE: Exactly. I try to do most things right, but this is one thing that's not perfect.	*Change talk ("I try to do most things right . . . "). Connection is improved further.*
COACH: Can I ask you, what might you do to get here on time?	*Switches to a <u>guiding</u> style with a key question that invites the athlete to solve the problem.*
ATHLETE: I'm not sure . . .	*Change talk.*
COACH: It could be hard for you to find a way.	*Listening statement.*
ATHLETE: I don't see it as such a big deal, to be honest, but yes, maybe I just go to bed too late and then it catches up with me in the morning.	*Change talk ("Maybe I just go to bed too late . . . ").*
COACH: You can see what might change.	*Athlete says "maybe" so the coach makes a listening statement with the word* might *that gives her the space to say how keen she is. It's up to her to confirm or clarify in some way.*
ATHLETE: Not sure, man, but I'll try going to bed earlier.	*Confirms this with stronger change talk.*
COACH: I wanted to let you in on my thinking on why I've raised this with you today. We had to delay our strategy discussion until you arrived. We can't function well as a unit until everyone comes to practice on time.	*Now the coach switches to a <u>fixing</u> style.*
ATHLETE: Sure, I get it, Coach.	*Athlete less defensive and now much more on board.*

Statement	What's going on?
COACH: Sometimes I'm forced to use sanctions like dropping people from the team, and this is the last thing I want to do with you.	*Having invested in following and then guiding first, the coach is now able to give a direct message to a much more receptive athlete.*
ATHLETE: Sure, thanks for saying that because I'm here to start every game. I'll do my best, Coach.	*Strong change talk ("I'll do my best . . . ").*

Notice how a fixing style is used at the end, after two key interventions: Connect with the player first using a *following* style; ask how the player might solve the problem using a *guiding* style; and then, if necessary, use a *fixing* style to lay out your expectations and directions for improved behavior.

By the time it came to using a fixing style and talking about sanctions like being dropped from the team, the athlete felt respected, less defensive, could see the bigger picture, and expressed change talk quite genuinely ("I'll do my best, Coach."). That specific style sequence (follow–guide–fix)

> Follow first, then guide. Then, only if needed, fix.

seemed to do the job better than if only a fixing style had been used. It might not always work out as easily as it did above, but you generally make better progress this way.

> **TIP:** *Don't leap in with a fixing style—use it when you have a good connection and can look for solutions together. Many times coaches who are able to "confront" effectively do so by building a strong relationship first and picking the right time and place to give feedback.*

Conclusion

When an athlete doesn't follow the rules, there is a big demand for you as a coach to immediately adopt a fixing style. After all, there is the sense that other coaches and the rest of the team is watching to see if and how you respond to a player who isn't responding to the rules. Something like showing up late for practice can be viewed as "bad behavior" in need of correction or even punishment, which might explain why a coach turns to a fixing style to eliminate the problem. This more effective strategy draws its fire from a different set of assumptions that can be more rewarding to use, and they often produce better outcomes: these individuals are people, not just athletes, and there are reasons for their behavior that warrant giving them a chance to express and consider changing. By resisting that righting reflex, the powerful urge to fix, you open the door for big, sustainable changes.

You might be wondering where MI fits into that conversation? It was right there in the space of a minute during which a guiding style was used. It started with that question "Can I ask you, what might you do to get here on time?" Such a useful, forward-looking key question is worth exploring the answer to, drawing out from athletes their own good reasons to change, and this is what the coach did, taking care not to divert the conversation in any way and using listening statements to give the athlete space to dig a little deeper into her own motivations ("It could be hard for you"). Slowly, as the athlete felt safe enough to be vulnerable, the change talk started to come out ("Maybe I just go to bed too late . . ."). You'll probably need more than one conversation to really turn things around, but this strategy at least gets you on the right path, using the idea that athletes might have the solution inside them.

> **TIP:** *Do athletes have the answer inside them to adapt their behavior or approach? Ask them. Assume they have the resources to make the changes.*

Martin Luther King once said, "The arc of the moral universe is long, but it bends towards justice." Your role as a coach is not to try to snap the arc of change into place; it's to help it bend, slowly. For MI to work well, your focus is on the athlete, and curiosity will beat cleverness every time.

Curiosity beats cleverness every time.

STRATEGY: ASSESS MOTIVATION

Summary: Assess and boost motivation in a single brief conversation. Ask athletes how much they really want to make a change on a scale of 1 to 10. Follow up with "scaling questions" that pull for positive change talk.

When you wonder how motivated an athlete is to make a specific change, or perhaps doubt whether he or she is fully committed, this is the time to consider this simple strategy. You'll find yourself moving beyond assessment into using MI itself within minutes, because the assessment invites athletes to say why and how they might change.

The Strategy in Action

You can be sure that the motivation to get up early, have a balanced diet, work on practice routines, develop this or that technique, get on better with fellow athletes—or whatever the focus—will vary across these different challenges, hence the value of being specific when you assess motivation. Consider this example of a coach discussing a change in technique with an athlete.

> COACH: How do you feel about making this change in your shooting technique?
>
> ATHLETE: Now I don't know, Coach. It sounds good, but it's a small change. And how comfortable will it be? I don't know.
>
> COACH: You remember how we used numbers last time, from 1 to 10, about how much you really want to do this, deep down? If 1 is not at all, and 10 is very keen, what's your number here?
>
> ATHLETE: Right in the middle, about a 5.
>
> COACH: So why a 5 and not 1 or 2?
>
> ATHLETE: Well, I definitely could improve my shooting, so why not give it a try, but I guess it's scary too, yeah. (*Laughs.*)
>
> COACH: What will help your number go up from 5 to 7 or even 8?
>
> ATHLETE: I tell you what. Give me a week to get over this next game and then we try in it practice, many times, and then we see how it looks, OK?

Here you are assessing motivation via a normal conversation. Not only that, you are also, via the scaling questions, using MI to help her say why and how she might change, in a very short time. Quick decision, better outcome? How did this come about?

Replay the Tape

Statement	What's going on?
COACH: How do you feel about making this change in your shooting technique?	*A simple open question initiates the assessment.*
ATHLETE: Now I don't know, Coach. It sounds good, but it's a small change. And how comfortable will it be? I don't know.	*The athlete is unsure.*

Statement	What's going on?
COACH: You remember how we used numbers last time, from 1 to 10, about how much you really want to do this, deep down? If 1 is not at all, and 10 is very keen, what's your number here?	*Starts the assessment. Asks a key question and for a rating on the scale from 1 to 10.*
ATHLETE: Right in the middle, about a 5.	*Gives herself a score.*
COACH: So why a 5 and not 1 or 2?	*Asks a key question that digs a little deeper and is designed to elicit change talk.*
ATHLETE: Well, I definitely could improve my shooting, so why not give it a try, but I guess it's scary too, yeah. (*Laughs.*)	*Athlete opens up with change talk.*
COACH: What will help your number go up from 5 to 7 or even 8?	*Another key question that looks up the scale, designed to elicit more change talk.*
ATHLETE: I tell you what. Give me a week to get over this next game and then we try in it practice, many times, and then we see how it looks, OK?	*Change talk and a plan emerges.*

Getting It Right

Here's a detailed summary of how this strategy can work:

1. *Ask about motivation to change.* A single question can unearth a goldmine of self-discovery for the athlete. When coaching, sometimes we layer questions, peppering athletes with several questions at once. Rather than asking several questions one after the other and potentially overloading athletes, focus on asking one efficient, curious, and pointed question. If the response is initially a silent one, it's usually because they are digging deep to find the answer, in which case avoid interrupting the silence. Nowhere is the wisdom of this guideline more apparent than with this strategy, so useful is the question you ask about motivation. It can be like lighting a warm fire—the athletes might have never thought about their sport like this before, and your task is then to gently blow into the fire, not smother it. What question? Consider any of these below:

"How important is it to you to make this change in technique?"
"How ready are you to . . . ?"

"How motivated are you to . . . ?"
"How much do you really want to . . . ?"

2. *Use a "ruler" to anchor the assessment.* You'll hear an answer of some kind, quite possibly an unclear one, and this is where a "ruler" with scaling questions can help a lot: Ask the athlete to imagine a scale from 1 to 10 for motivation (1 = very low, 10 = very high), and then simply ask, "What number would you give yourself?" You'll seldom get an answer at an extreme end of the rating scale, a 1 or a 10. It's more often something in between. Imagine that the answer is 5, a common expression of uncertainty in which voices for and against change simultaneously lower and lift the athlete's motivation to change (see Chapter 3).

3. *Use MI to boost motivation.* Having secured a judgment from athletes about their motivation, the door is now open to using MI in the easiest way we know of, to draw their own good reasons to change. In fact, there are two doors, and you can go through both of them quite quickly. One question looks back down the scale, the other up the scale toward higher motivation. In each case the answer you receive will be change talk. With the first question that looks back down the scale, they tell you why they are motivated right now, while with the second question that looks up the scale, they tell you what will help them get fired up to become more motivated.

> "Why did you give yourself a 5 and not a lower number like a 1 or 2 . . . not very motivated?" The answer will be change talk (reasons it is important to change), such as "I know this is a good plan that I change how I use my hands here."
> "What would help the number go up from a 5 to 7 or 8?"

Whichever question you ask, the answer will be change talk. It's well worth continuing to listen at this point because you will be able to use MI to boost motivation further.

Conclusion

Passing negative judgment about someone's motivation is a common pastime, often associated with frustration about what is going to really help him or her to improve. In the absence of a real understanding of what's up with the person, the judgments can become too broad and even rigid; for example:, "She's simply not motivated, and she's like this most the time." The strategy above allows you to explore an athlete's motivation in a more helpful way, by viewing it as something that can and does change. You ask them and help them to find ways to lift their own motivation.

> **TIP:** *Try to avoid making judgments about motivation—rather ask the athlete. Motivation is seldom black or white, and it changes a lot over time.*

STRATEGY: THE "WHY" AND "HOW" OF CHANGE

Summary: Dig a little deeper into low motivation by asking about "why" and "how" they might change their approach or behavior. The athletes will do the motivating for themselves. If motivation were a battery, flagging motivation would be a signal that it is running low.

> "I wish I could get better, but I just can't."
> "I don't want to go to practice so often."
> "I'm not sure I can do it."
> "I'm losing it for some reason."
> "I think I have had enough of this sport."
> "I don't want to leave the club, but I must get on with my life."

Coaches often focus on *how* athletes might reach their goals and what the target is and how to get there, and they miss a golden opportunity to consider *why* it might be important. This strategy tackles both of these drivers of motivation. We sometimes put it like this: MOTIVATION = WHY + HOW. Ignore the "WHY" and you might miss where the problem lies. Instead of solving the motivational problem for the athletes, MI helps them to do this for themselves. Here's an example of the strategy in use with an athlete who says something like "the practice sessions aren't going well."

MOTIVATION = WHY + HOW.

The Strategy in Action

It's one thing to observe a problem of low motivation or doubt, another to make a difference in conversation. This strategy is almost failsafe and provides a direct route to exploring motivation, where you help an athlete to dig a little deeper with a simple aim: The athlete—rather than you—talks about *why* and *how* change might come about. How might you do this efficiently? See what you make of this next example, where a coach notices that things have not gone so well in practice. The athlete seems to be low on energy and motivation, and trying too hard at the same time.

COACH: If we step back from today, how are you feeling about your progress over the last few months?

ATHLETE: Not so good. To be honest, Coach, the practice sessions aren't going well.

COACH: I want to ask you two questions, and the first one is this: How *important* is it for you to practice regularly?

ATHLETE: Yes and no . . . it's just not going well at the moment.

COACH: If I ask you to give me a number, where 1 is not at all important and 10 is very important, what number would you give yourself for how important it is for you right now to practice regularly?

ATHLETE: About an 8.

COACH: Can I ask you, why an 8 and not a lower number like 4 or 5?

ATHLETE: Oh, that's easy. I want to do better; you know me: this sport is my life at the moment. It's my number 1 priority, and I am determined to do better.

COACH: You want to get better times.

ATHLETE: Oh, for sure. They must get better.

COACH: Now to that second question: How *confident* do you feel about practicing regularly to get those better times?

ATHLETE: It's not working at the moment. I'm tired a lot, and I don't feel good afterward. I don't know what's wrong.

COACH: Something is not working out for you at the moment.

ATHLETE: Am I practicing too much or something?

COACH: You've been wondering about that.

ATHLETE: Well, why am I so tired? I must be pushing myself and getting drained out.

COACH: The balance is not quite right for you.

ATHLETE: No way; it's all out of balance. Things aren't easy at home, but that's no big deal; I'm used to lots going on at home.

COACH: If 1 was not all confident and 10 was very confident about finding that balance and practicing just right, what number would you give yourself right now?

ATHLETE: About a 5. I am worried that if I practice less, I'll lose form.

COACH: Why did you give yourself a 5 and not a 1?

ATHLETE: (*Hesitates.*) I've had times when it's all going well, so I remember what it's like. I must be able to find that again.

COACH: You really want to get this right.

ATHLETE: Oh, for sure, I *must* get it right.

COACH: What's going to help you get from a 5 to a 6, 7, or even 8?

ATHLETE: I've been there before, and I must get there. Maybe I should keep track of my practice and write down a note of how tired I feel when I get up, and before and after practice, and the number of hours I put in.

COACH: Can I add some advice in here that I've found to be helpful for other athletes in your position? (*Coach waits for athlete to agree with a nod.*) Consider also whether you might want to do a more radical experiment—drop the number of hours for a week or so, and note in your diary what happens to your energy. It's up to you. What do you think makes the most sense?

Replay the Tape

Statement	What's going on?
COACH: If we step back from today, how are you feeling about your progress over the last few months?	
ATHLETE: Not so good. To be honest, Coach, the practice sessions aren't going well.	
COACH: I want to ask you two questions, and the first one is this: How *important* is it for you to practice regularly?	*Key question.*
ATHLETE: Yes and no . . . it's just not going well at the moment.	
COACH: If I ask you to give me a number, where 1 is not at all important and 10 is very important, what number would you give yourself for how important it is for you right now to practice regularly?	*Asks for a number.*
ATHLETE: About an 8.	
COACH: Can I ask you, why an 8 and not a lower number, like 4 or 5?	

Statement	What's going on?
ATHLETE: Oh, that's easy. I want to do better; you know me: this sport is my life at the moment. It's my number 1 priority, and I am determined to do better.	*Strong change talk.*
COACH: You want to get better times.	*Listening statement designed to encourage more change talk.*
ATHLETE: Oh, for sure. They must get better.	*Change talk.*
COACH: Now to that second question: How *confident* do you feel about practicing regularly to get those better times?	
ATHLETE: It's not working at the moment. I'm tired a lot, and I don't feel good afterward. I don't know what's wrong.	
COACH: Something is not working out for you at the moment.	*Listening statement.*
ATHLETE: Am I practicing too much or something?	
COACH: You've been wondering about that.	*Uses listening statement to encourage athlete to answer it.*
ATHLETE: Well, why am I so tired? I must be pushing myself and getting drained out.	
COACH: The balance is not quite right for you.	*Listening statement designed to dig a little deeper.*
ATHLETE: No way; it's all out of balance. Things aren't easy at home, but that's no big deal; I'm used to lots going on at home.	
COACH: If 1 was not all confident and 10 was very confident about finding that balance and practicing just right, what number would you give yourself right now?	*Asks a key question and calls for a rating.*
ATHLETE: About a 5. I am worried that if I practice less, I'll lose form.	

Statement	What's going on?
COACH: Why did you give yourself a 5 and not a 1?	
ATHLETE: (*Hesitates.*) I've had times when it's all going well, so I remember what it's like. I must be able to find that again.	*Change talk.*
COACH: You really want to get this right.	*Listening statement.*
ATHLETE: Oh, for sure, I *must* get it right.	*Stronger change talk.*
COACH: What's going to help you get from a 5 to a 6, 7, or even 8?	*Key question looking up the scale and designed to elicit more change talk.*
ATHLETE: I've been there before, and I must get there. Maybe I should keep track of my practice and write down a note of how tired I feel when I get up, and before and after practice, and the number of hours I put in.	*Change talk.*
COACH: Can I add some advice in here that I've found to be helpful for other athletes in your position? (*Coach waits for athlete to agree with a nod.*) Consider also whether you might want to do a more radical experiment—drop the number of hours for a week or so, and note in your diary what happens to your energy. It's up to you. What do you think makes the most sense?	*Offers advice on the back of good connection; asks permission; uses language that encourages choice and champions autonomy ("consider," "might want to," "what do you think makes the most sense?"). See Chapter 10.*

There are two key questions in that sequence, and no two athletes answer them the same. One is about the "why" or importance of change; the other is about the "how" or confidence to achieve it. The first gives athletes space to talk about their values and what's in their hearts; the second, to address effort, confidence, and techniques for improving practice or performance. In either case they—rather than you—take the lead, and it's one of the most direct routes we know to drawing out change talk from athletes.

Our experience of many conversations using this strategy is that the first "why" question can often get overlooked in favor of the second "how" question, which is more focused on action. We usually ask about the "why" first, because it gives the athletes space to affirm their values, like charging up a motivation battery. Also, sometimes the "why" is where the problem lies, and it helps an athlete to address this in a safe space with someone they trust.

TIP: *Ask about the "why" of change before asking about "how" an athlete might achieve it. This usually brings rewards.*

Another golden rule we use is to listen like crazy when asking about either "why" or "how." Here's an example from that exchange above:

ATHLETE: Am I practicing too much or something?

COACH: You've been wondering about that. [listening statement]

ATHLETE: Well, why am I so tired? I must be pushing myself and getting drained out.

This was MI at its best—simple and very brief, where a listening statement pulled out the athlete's answer to her own question.

TIP: *After asking a key question, use listening statements to draw answers from the athlete.*

The scaling questions and requests for numerical ratings merely provide the scaffold for generating this positive talk about change, when athletes express the motivation that's already inside them. While scaling rulers are not distinct to MI, using them strategically with skillful listening can make them a useful tool for building engagement and change talk.

Getting It Right

We have worked and reworked this strategy and observed its practice in many settings. Here are the guidelines we use in training:

ASK TWO OPEN QUESTIONS ABOUT CHANGE

"How *important* is it for you to make this change?" ("Why?")

Follow the question for a while with a curious attitude and belief that the answer is inside the athletes. Listening statements will help you move forward. All kinds of answers will emerge, including negative ones, and yet athletes usually include positive reasons for change, such as "I need to do it because . . ."; "I must do it . . ."; "I want to because . . ."; and so on. Then ask the second question.

"How *confident* do you feel about succeeding?" ("How?")

Repeat the above; you'll hear about the challenges and how the athletes feel about overcoming them. This will likely include positive statements about their confidence, such as "I think I can do it if I just focus and practice."

SUMMARIZE

Pause at this point. Where does the main challenge lie, with the why or the how? See if you can summarize how athletes feel about both questions—for example: "So you are not sure you can succeed with this change because of _____, and yet you also feel it's important, that it will improve your game and help you to _____." Capture the positives in this summary, if possible.

ASK A KEY QUESTION ABOUT CHANGE

"What do you think you will do?"
"What's best for you right now?"
"What is the next step as you see it?"

This is a critical moment when the athlete might well make a decision, and it's much better for this decision to be based on their own wisdom about what's best, rather than yours.

USE RULERS TO SUPPORT THE CONVERSATION

When you ask those two key questions, about the why and the how, here's a summary of how you can use rulers and numbers to structure the conversation. You ask questions about their scores that help them to say either why or how they might move forward. We've seen this used in all settings with the rulers drawn on a piece of paper.

"How *important* is it for you to make this change? Can I ask you to give me a number, say from 1 to 10, where 1 is not at all important and 10 is very important? What number would you give yourself right now?"

The score will seldom be either 1 or 10. Let's say it is 6. Then consider either of these two questions:

"Why did you give yourself a score of 6 and not 1?"

The answer will be about them telling you why change is important, what we called "change talk" in Chapter 1.

"What do you need for that score to go up from 6 to say 7 or 8?"

Again, the athletes will tell you what will lift their motivation to change.

"How *confident* do you feel about succeeding?"

You can now do exactly what was done above with importance. For example, if the athlete scores 3, you could ask this:

"Why did you give yourself a score of 3 and not 1?"

The answer will be about what confidence they have inside them.

"What do you need for that score to go up from 3 to say 4 or 5?"

The athletes will tell you what will lift their confidence to change.

Conclusion

Flexibility is key when using this strategy. One athlete will be so locked into lack of confidence and the "how" of change that you will focus only on this, perhaps with a ruler and numbers, and not on the importance or "why" of change. With others, it might be the reverse. Some people thrive with rulers, others less so. You can practice this in any situation where you have a good connection with an athlete, and decide to spend a few minutes digging down into how they might change.

A CONVERSATION THAT LIFTS MOTIVATION

As you try out this kind of conversation, notice how you sometimes enter a zone that athletes know well: there is no distraction, just pure concentration. You don't always get into the zone, let alone stay in it, but when you do, change and improvement happens because you are both moving forward together.

In some ways practice *is* our moment to shine as coaches. Many coaches feel that once the team is on the field or court, "The hay is in the barn." That is, the real work in preparing the players has already happened. Our opportunities to connect and fuel the individuals and the team as a whole lie in these moments to practice connecting and drawing out the "why" and "how" of change. This selection of strategies is an invitation to practice MI, knowing that you will do no harm and that you will get better as you slip into this simple "groove" with the athletes telling you why and how they might change. As you do so, you'll get immediate feedback from them about how well you are doing. If they talk freely, you know you are getting it right. If they resist, you've overshot the mark somehow—in which case, reconnect and proceed once again. Practice is like that. It never really makes you perfect, but you do, as they say, become more consistent.

QUESTIONS TO CONSIDER

- How can you lift motivation each practice?
- How can you help players feel more involved in routines they see as boring and repetitive? Could you ask them this question?
- Think about a change in your life that you feel you should make but are struggling with. You are about to speak with someone you trust about this. What would you like and not like in the conversation?

CHAPTER 9

Setting Goals
and Making Plans

Don't start without my heart.
—19-YEAR-OLD ATHLETE

HIGHLIGHTS

+ Strategies: (1) Connect and assess; (2) the "why" of goal setting; (3) the "how" of goal setting; (4) the "what" of goal setting.

+ When you hear change talk, reflect it with more listening statements.

Goal setting can be improved by using MI skills to draw out what's really important to athletes and devise a shared plan that makes sense to them. As their change talk emerges, encourage them to say more, to spell out why, what, and how they might improve. Their plan is yours too.

THE KICKOFF

If you set a goal with an athlete, what percentage of the time do they take up, execute, and stick with the plan that was made? Is it 50 to 60%? That's quite common, especially in team sports. Between this estimate and an improved hit rate lies the opportunity to consider how MI might help you improve your skills and their performance.

One common mistake is to put the cart before the horse, to focus on *what* to do and *how* before adequately considering *why*. Another challenge is home territory for MI: How do you help athletes take ownership of and be motivated to identify their goals and stay committed to the steps for reaching them?

FROM THE FRONTLINE

It is the beginning of a new tennis season, and Annette, one of your most talented players, walks up to you and spontaneously tells you that she "needs to get better" at some important aspect of her play. Excitedly, you give her some advice about how she could improve her mechanics and timing. You suggest a goal for what she could achieve with this adjustment and are feeling optimistic about her reaching that target. In the next match, you are surprised to see that she isn't putting any of the good pointers you made to use. In fact, it seems as if the entire conversation that you had with her has gone in one ear and out the other.

All sorts of things can go wrong with goal planning. In this chapter we look at how you can use your relationship and MI to best effect. Is it wise for the best ideas to always come from the coach? The special place of MI in sports is in the way you use your relationship to get the athlete to come up with new ideas, supported by your expertise, not dominated by it. *How* you set goals might be just as important as what they are. This chapter uses a "why, what, and how" framework as a guide. We chose this scheme because it is closely connected to how MI works best, as you will see below.

It probably goes back to our hunter-gatherer days, the idea that if we have a clear plan in mind we will be more likely to succeed, especially if we work on and review it with others. Then another requirement is flexibility, essential too, because as soon as you make a plan, things change. You might say with some conviction to an athlete, "Follow this goal; let's keep going" and then it turns out a bit different.

> How you set goals is as important as what they are.

WHY, WHAT, AND HOW

These three words—"why," "what," and "how"—have been widely used to improve goal setting and performance, from the early work in the 1970s by Gerard Egan on skilled helping (see Egan, 2013) to more recent applications in the field of leadership (see Sinek, 2011). With athletes, the relevance is clear enough: First up is to understand what they most need to unblock their road to improvement and then work on one or more of the why, what, and how of goal setting. The *why* is often critical.

It is often a good idea to assess the best way forward (see Figure 9.1). Of course, because athlete needs vary so much, you will not always need to go rigidly through the sequence of tasks presented in Figure 9.1. However, if motivation seems to block athletes' efforts to make the change, it is often because their hearts are not in it and the question about "why?" has not been adequately addressed.

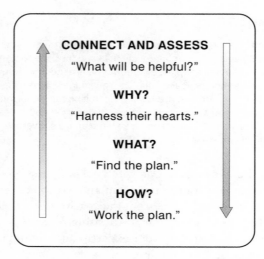

FIGURE 9.1. Key tasks in goal setting with MI.

STRATEGY: CONNECT AND ASSESS

Summary: What does the athlete need? Where's the blockage? Is there a need to address why, how, or what? Is the athlete confused, uncertain about succeeding, or wanting to set a different goal? Have the conversation to clarify things.

> **TIP:** *If things are not clear, ask the athlete.*

That story about Annette above was about tennis, but it could have been almost any sport. Why did the plan not work? Was it a bad night's sleep, a competitor reaching a higher level, bad luck, lack of confidence, or what? Did the coach perhaps dominate the process and undermine her ownership of the plan?

The Strategy in Action

COACH: Hi, Annette. Can we have a chat about how you are getting on?

ANNETTE: Hi, sure. It's been a tough week.

COACH: Even though you lost that match, you fought hard for sure.

ANNETTE: Thanks, Coach. I was down afterward, but I nearly had her in the second set.

COACH: You got that close.

ANNETTE: Nearly, but not good enough, and then I think I lost my focus at a critical point there, and wham, she came back at me so hard I couldn't cope.

COACH: You can see where you might have lost it.

ANNETTE: Exactly, Coach. We see it the same way.

COACH: Can I ask you what happened to that goal we set for you, the one about coming into the net more?

ANNETTE: I knew you would ask me about that. It was a nice idea, but I just froze and didn't feel confident enough to do it. My weight was on the back foot, and I never found the time to rush forward.

COACH: It's something you want to do, if only you can make it happen.

ANNETTE: Maybe we can practice it now this week; if I can do it more, it will help for sure.

COACH: You'd like to try it out.

ANNETTE: Yes, this goal was a good one. I just need to commit to it big time and have a go.

Replay the Tape

Statement	What's going on?
COACH: Hi, Annette. Can we have a chat about how you are getting on?	*Asking permission. Coach plans to connect first above all else.*
ANNETTE: Hi, sure. It's been a tough week.	
COACH: Even though you lost that match, you fought hard for sure.	*Starts with a positive affirmation about fighting hard.*
ANNETTE: Thanks, Coach. I was down afterward, but I nearly had her in the second set.	*Responds positively and highlights her own memory of doing well.*
COACH: You got that close.	*Uses a simple listening statement to capture what happened and hand the conversation lead back to Annette.*

Statement	What's going on?
ANNETTE: Nearly, but not good enough, and then I think I lost my focus at a critical point there, and wham, she came back at me so hard I couldn't cope.	*She clarifies where she thinks she went wrong.*
COACH: You can see where you might have lost it.	*Another simple listening statement.*
ANNETTE: Exactly, Coach. We see it the same way.	*Annette confirms the accuracy of the coach's listening statement. The connection is clear and rapidly established.*
COACH: Can I ask you what happened to that goal we set for you, the one about coming into the net more?	*With a good connection made, the coach decides to ask about what happened to the goal they set. This is an informal assessment through conversation.*
ANNETTE: I knew you would ask me about that. It was a nice idea, but I just froze and didn't feel confident enough to do it. My weight was on the back foot, and I never found the time to rush forward.	*She describes what happened.*
COACH: It's something you want to do, if only you can make it happen.	*This is a guess, about her motivation, but the coach throws it out there for Annette to confirm or clarify in some way.*
ANNETTE: Maybe we can practice it now this week; if I can do it more, it will help for sure.	*Annette confirms this with change talk.*
COACH: You'd like to try it out.	*Annette said "maybe," so the coach makes a listening statement that gives her the space to say how keen she is.*
ANNETTE: Yes, this goal was a good one. I just need to commit to it big time and have a go.	*She confirms with stronger change talk an intention to try it out.*

Conclusion

Goal setting is a very human process, and your relationship can sit center stage when you connect first and then give the athlete the chance to be vulnerable and open up about how things are going. The assessment is as much about establishing feelings as it might be about zooming in on facts and strategies.

> **TIP:** *Help them to feel safe and share vulnerability—this will promote more reliable assessment and better goal planning.*

STRATEGY: THE "WHY" OF GOAL SETTING

Summary: Is motivation flagging? Might they need to remind themselves about what they really want and why this goal is important to them? Use the "why" of goal-setting strategy to help them say what's important.

You can run all the wisdom of science and technical knowledge past an athlete, but behind that sits their heart, their values, their motivation—and doubt as well. This is where MI can help you to merge goal setting with what makes good sense to the athlete as a person. If they feel safe speaking with you, and if they know why they are doing something, ideally connected to their deeper personal values, then the heart and the head can unite, and you can keep it this way as you work through with them the steps needed to achieve their goals.

FROM THE FRONTLINE

Anna Botha is in her late 70s and the coach of a world champion. Self-taught, in a remote corner of the world, Namibia, she coached Frankie Fredericks, the multiple world and Olympic sprint champion, and now works in South Africa with a group that includes her star performer, Wayde van Niekerk, current world and Olympic record holder for the 400-meter sprint. How does she do it? Her answers are consistent and clear: "If you see your athletes as machines, I don't think you will have the satisfaction of feeling that you achieved something. It has to be about helping another human being reach these goals and dreams."

The idea of harnessing the power of an individual's heart can be powerful. You don't see goal setting as a purely logical task, but go with their heart, their love of sports, and their true values. If we align our sails with that wind, progress is more assured in propelling them toward their goals. Any of these key questions below can help you get started.

Key Questions

"What goal do you want to aim for?"

This is like holding a mirror up for athletes to look into. It's a good opportunity to connect and listen. Asking this question shows athletes that you see them as people, not just athletes. Tune into what lifts the heart, what they value, like, and enjoy. Keep the goal personal and proximal, within their control. Expect to hear change talk, and use listening statements that lift their motivation further.

Other useful questions: "What is achievable and will improve your performance?"; "What's going to really fire you up?"; "What will help you to be your best?" An unclear picture is also OK—no need to have complete clarity all at once.

"Why is this goal important to you?"

This is a direct route into personal values. It's rewarding to stay on this path and not get diverted into premature planning. You'll notice strengths—highlight them.

Other useful questions: "What does this goal really mean for you?"; "What will achieving this mean to you?"; "When you achieve this goal, what will happen for you?" Sometimes it is necessary to prompt athletes with a phrase, such as "tell me more," or a question, such as "And why is that important to you?" to really connect to their underlying values.

"How ready do you feel?"

Being not quite ready is a common reason for failure. Notice the change talk that reflects how committed they are. If in doubt, check it out with the athletes.

Other useful questions: "How much do you really want to head in this direction?"; "What will help you to feel more prepared/ready?"; "How can I help you to feel more ready?" Asking questions like these helps athletes to take charge of the goal-setting process. Otherwise, as coaches, we are simply guessing at what will help them, like aiming for a target with our eyes closed.

The Strategy in Action

Just because an athlete says yes to a goal does not imply 100% commitment. "Harnessing the heart" can be a useful way of building motivation, because a person says *why* a goal is important. To say these things in front of someone else is to share personal dreams and vulnerabilities in a special way, a privilege for any coach to hear and be part of. It's also more likely to predict sticking to the goal and working hard to achieve it. In Annette's case below, the coach chooses to simply start a conversation asking, "Why is this goal important to you?"

> COACH: We talked this morning about trying out this goal of coming into the net more, but before we get into when and how, can I ask you *why* this goal is important to you?
>
> ANNETTE: Ha ha. (*Laughs.*) To win more games of course, but seriously, I've been punished for trying this in the past so I have not tried it for ages.
>
> COACH: It hasn't worked out that well, yet somehow you think it might be useful to work on now.
>
> ANNETTE: Ah, that's because I don't want to stagnate as a player. I want to keep developing new things as I get older.
>
> COACH: You still feel you have more to learn.
>
> ANNETTE: I'll tell you how I feel: Once I feel I can't learn any more, well, that's really depressing. I sacrifice so much for this sport. I owe it to myself to work like mad on improving my technique.
>
> COACH: You want to get some new energy into your game with techniques to match.
>
> ANNETTE: Exactly right.
>
> COACH: So let me ask you, Where did you get stuck with this coming into the net after we spoke last time?

Replay the Tape

Statement	What's going on?
COACH: We talked this morning about trying out this goal of coming into the net more, but before we get into when and how, can I ask you *why* this goal is important to you?	*Decides to "harness the heart" and ask the "why" question (see "Key Questions" above).*
ANNETTE: Ha ha. (*Laughs.*) To win more games of course, but seriously, I've been punished for trying this in the past so I have not tried it for ages.	*She talks about her doubts.*

Statement	What's going on?
COACH: It hasn't worked out that well, yet somehow you think it might be useful to work on now.	*Listening statement.*
ANNETTE: Ah, that's because I don't want to stagnate as a player. I want to keep developing new things as I get older.	*She talks about her personal values—change talk is emerging ("I want to . . . ").*
COACH: You still feel you have more to learn.	*A listening statement that reflects positive change talk designed to capture how she might be feeling.*
ANNETTE: I'll tell you how I feel: Once I feel I can't learn any more, well, that's really depressing. I sacrifice so much for this sport. I owe it to myself to work like mad on improving my technique.	*Strong expression of personal values—more change talk ("I owe it to myself . . . ").*
COACH: You want to get some new energy into your game with techniques to match.	*Another listening statement designed to capture how she might be feeling.*
ANNETTE: Exactly right.	*Annette confirms the accuracy of the coach's summary.*
COACH: So let me ask you, Where did you get stuck with this coming into the net after we spoke last time?	*The coach decides to shift focus now to the goal itself.*

Conclusion

There are many key questions you can ask that tap into athletes' hearts and clarify why they want to achieve or set a goal. In the above example, just one question was used ("Can I ask you *why* this goal is important to you?"). Because the coach focused only on listening, with a clear mind free of clutter (see Chapter 8 on rapid connecting), Annette felt safe enough to explore the answer and express change talk. MI involves responding to this change talk by reflecting it back and encouraging the athlete to say more.

An athlete's saying
yes does not
ensure commitment.

TIP: *When you hear change talk, don't change the subject; reflect it with more listening statements.*

STRATEGY: THE "WHAT" OF GOAL SETTING

Summary: Is the athlete ready and motivated to set a goal and make a plan? There is probably more than one goal that might be helpful. A range of open guiding questions will help you to find the right one.

"Overcoaching" is frequently reported in sports these days, where coaches rather than athletes themselves set the pace and make the plans for change. Using MI, this need not happen because the athletes often have the answer inside them about what's best. What might this look like?

> COACH: What goal will make the most sense to you?
>
> ATHLETE: I want to try out that switch of hands at the right moment. [change talk]
>
> COACH: You want that to work for you. [listening statement]
>
> ATHLETE: I can definitely see myself doing that. [stronger change talk]
>
> COACH: Tell me how it will be?
>
> ATHLETE: Well, I'm going to choose my moment tomorrow and. . . . [more change talk]

Relying on the athlete's own ideas does not mean yours are irrelevant—it's more like the two of you putting ideas out on a table between you and leaving it to the athlete to say what will help the most; as you notice positive change talk, it's a signal worth reinforcing because it often sparks athletes into action. Here are some key open questions that can start off the search for the right plan.

> *Relying on the athlete's ideas does not make yours irrelevant.*

Key Questions

"What's the best way for you to reach this goal?"

The heart of goal setting. Map possible routes together. Help the athlete select the route that feels important and manageable. Narrow it down to precise details if possible. Notice and reinforce change talk.

Other useful questions: "How will this work out in practice?"; "What's the first step you could take?"; "What has helped you in the past?"; "What other steps will help?"; "How confident do you feel about succeeding?"; "How will you know it's working?"

"Can I offer you an idea?"

Offering, rather than imposing, your ideas frees athletes to make up their own minds (see Chapter 4).

Other useful questions: "I wonder whether it will help if. . . ."; "What do you think about . . . ?"; "I have an idea that has been very helpful to other athletes in your position. How would you feel if I shared it with you now?"

"How committed are you to this plan?"

Saying how committed they are increases their commitment! If there's doubt, ask them why.

Other useful questions: "What's going to help you really get going?"; "What would help you really take this plan with you on the field?"; "Just so I know we're on the same page here, how would you describe your plan?"

The Strategy in Action

Here's a brief example with an athlete who says he wants to try something new: change the way he prepares for action. In this case it's about using a breathing exercise before heading out into competition.

COACH: This game has its pressures, and you said you would like to try something new.

ATHLETE: For sure, I head out there when I'm up to bat, and my head is sometimes spinning I am so fired up.

COACH: You want to be a little calmer.

ATHLETE: No, not really; I want to be more focused, not necessarily calmer, like I want to be in the zone with no distractions.

COACH: So what's the best way for you to get into that zone?

ATHLETE: I spoke to Zane, and he does this breathing thing before he goes out that could really help me.

COACH: So that's the goal for you, and you want to try it out.

ATHLETE: Yes, it should make a difference.

COACH: So how exactly might you do this?

ATHLETE: I learn the breathing thing and then use it on my own quietly before I head out, but it will need to work with just a minute of preparation.

COACH: Can I suggest a way of doing this? See what you think about this. . . . (*Explains, providing options.*)

Replay the Tape

Statement	What's going on?
COACH: This game has its pressures, and you said you would like to try something new.	
ATHLETE: For sure, I head out there when I'm up to bat, and my head is sometimes spinning I am so fired up.	*States the problem.*
COACH: You want to be a little calmer.	*A guess in the form of a listening statement.*
ATHLETE: No, not really; I want to be more focused, not necessarily calmer, like I want to be in the zone with no distractions.	*The guess was not quite accurate so the athlete clarifies.*
COACH: So what's the best way for you to get into that zone?	*Open question to find the goal.*
ATHLETE: I spoke to Zane, and he does this breathing thing before he goes out that could really help me.	*Presents an idea with change talk (" . . . that could really help me").*
COACH: So that's the goal for you, and you want to try it out.	*Listening statement reflecting change talk.*
ATHLETE: Yes, it should make a difference.	*Change talk.*
COACH: So how exactly might you do this?	*Open question to find the plan.*
ATHLETE: I learn the breathing thing and then use it on my own quietly before I head out, but it will need to work with just a minute of preparation.	*Change talk.*
COACH: Can I suggest a way of doing this? See what you think about this. . . . (*Explains, providing options.*) [See Chapter 10 on giving advice.]	

Conclusion

This common kind of conversation is strongly influenced by MI in that the goal-setting process involves reinforcing the athlete's ideas as they come up, using simple open questions (e.g., "So what's the best way for you to get into that zone?") and listening statements that reinforce change talk as it arises (e.g., "So that's the goal for you, and you want to try it out"). There's no formula for goal planning, hence the list of key questions for you to choose from, or make up others yourself, all based on your curiosity about what might work for the athlete.

> **TIP:** *Choose a useful key question and then follow the search for an answer.*

STRATEGY: THE "HOW" OF GOAL SETTING

Summary: The goal is clear, and it's a question of exactly what's the best execution method to "work the plan." Details will matter. Commitment will be important too, and you can pick this up in the strength of athletes' change talk, which you encourage as much as possible.

Learning from victories and mistakes is at the heart of progress. Doing this together is where MI skills can really help.

Key Questions

Timing is everything: We have known great coaches who say it is less about the exact questions you ask and more about when you ask them. Some athletes want to talk about their performance directly after the competition. Some would prefer to examine things after a good night's sleep. Observing and thinking about individual differences will help you to time your open questions in a way that will improve how effective they are.

"How's it going?"

This is a time to share their experience and your observations. Listen and connect without interruption to begin with. How happy is the athlete with this plan? Assuming progress is reasonable, what adjustments might be helpful? Avoid too much problem talk. Ask positive questions about how improvement might come about.

Other useful questions: "What are your top two ideas for improvement?"; "What worked best there?"; "What have you seen others do that has worked here?"; "Which of your top strengths can you bring in here?"; "Can you see the solution in your mind, or should we make time for imagining it?"; "What do you need from me right now that would be helpful?"

"Can I suggest . . . ?"

Connect first, provide choice, and allow athletes to reach conclusions about the implications for them (see Chapter 10 on advice giving).

"**Ready to go?**"

Check for commitment—for example: "How committed are you to this plan?"; and "How ready do you feel to try again?" Questions like these are all designed to elicit change talk; reinforce it with further listening statements, and commitment will get stronger.

The Strategy in Action (A Coach's Goal Setting)

How might a failed plan be turned around? Here's the captain of a softball team worried about her leadership after a series of defeats. Her coach and she agreed on this goal: "I want to have 5 to 10 minutes with the team during the postmatch reviews so I can connect better with them, hear their concerns, and make my expectations clear as well." It didn't work well. The more she spoke, the less they did. Afterward, they reviewed the plan.

COACH: How do you feel it went?

ATHLETE: Disaster! They never said a thing, and I just panicked and spoke all the time. Dumb idea if ever there was one. (*Laughs nervously.*)

COACH: You tried something new there, and wow, you had to be brave in the face of their silence.

ATHLETE: You can say that again. I guess I learned what not to do. (*Laughs nervously.*)

COACH: Was the goal maybe a little ambitious, or would you like to try some ways of improving the meetings?

ATHLETE: No, I just can't see it working well right now; maybe it's just too formal, these team meetings.

COACH: You want to connect better with them and hear their concerns, but you are wondering whether the meeting is the right place to do it.

ATHLETE: Exactly. I want to keep that overall goal of communicating better with them. [So the goal is adjusted a little.]

COACH: What might work better to achieve this?

ATHLETE: I am better in less formal situations, so why don't I use that asset?

COACH: How might you do that?

ATHLETE: I just strike up conversations with them anytime it seems right and listen to their concerns?

COACH: That might be more manageable.

ATHLETE: I bet it is. I can start tomorrow.

COACH: In a week or so we'll know how well it's going, this plan.

ATHLETE: Exactly. We review this in about a week from now. Meanwhile, I will give this plan a real go.

Conclusion

Well before that last conversation took place, there were others that must have allowed the athlete to feel safe and willing to express vulnerability about failure. In other words, the coach had taken time to connect with the athlete before goal setting was initiated. Then the coach was able to work the plan by using a guiding style to look at how things might improve and MI skills to draw out the wisdom about the next best step from the athlete, reinforcing change talk as it emerged. The relationship was the glue that held it all together. They effectively conducted an experiment, and its failure was seen not as a disaster but an opportunity to learn, with the coach using MI skills to let the athlete say what the next step might be.

TIP: *Conduct experiments, and encourage athletes to say why and how they might improve further.*

It was a measure of her strengths of character that she started the conversation with her coach, not by blaming herself for being a bad leader, but by laughing at herself and a plan that hadn't worked: "Dumb idea if ever there was one."

USING YOUR RELATIONSHIP

Some goals are concrete and easy to formulate, others are more personal, and it takes a little time to unravel what the athlete would like to aim for, why, and how to make progress. Either way, your relationship will be important. We talk about using the athlete's heartfelt desires as a platform for goal setting. If they sense that your heart is also really committed to the process, which you can demonstrate by staying in an MI style, the outcome is more likely to be satisfying and successful. MI skills are really there to give you the tools to make this journey together.

Heartfelt desires: the platform for goal setting.

QUESTIONS TO CONSIDER

- How many of your practice routines are done just because "that's the way it's always done around here"?

- What are the two to three things you would like to get better at in your work in sports? What plans are you making to improve on these things?

CHAPTER 10

Giving Advice and Feedback

The most important thing a coach does is give feedback.
—BOB BOWMAN, coach of swimmer Michael Phelps

HIGHLIGHTS

+ Connect first before giving feedback.
+ The more you respect athletes' choice of whether they take your advice, the more likely they are to take your advice.
+ Listening after giving advice is often the key to unlocking the athlete's courage to make the change you advise. That's where the usefulness of MI kicks in.
+ *Strategy:* ask–offer–ask. You ask first, then give advice, and then ask again what they make of it.

It's not just your technical knowledge that's important when giving feedback and advice. How you do this can make all the difference. There's an alternative strategy to instilling advice into athletes in which they take a much more active role in the whole process. It's easy to grasp and can be practiced in any situation, with individual athletes and in teams. That's the focus of this chapter.

THE KICKOFF

A casual observer might wonder whether the ultimate dream of all coaches is to have a telepathic connection to the brains of their athletes that allows a coach to see a problem, ping the message across to the athlete, and then sit back and enjoy the outcome. The problem of course is that athletes are people, each with their own quirky ways of looking at things, and few of them learn best by having information dumped into their brains. In the end, like it or not, they make their own sense of what's best to do. It's probably for this reason that author and raconteur Terry Pratchett apparently once said, "After all, when I go for advice, I don't really want them to give it; I just want them to be there while I talk to myself." People can often give themselves their own best advice, what we call "change talk" in MI. So what does make for effective, athlete-centered advice giving? How much training were you given in *how* to do this?

This chapter describes a single, simple strategy (ask–offer–ask) that we developed alongside MI that champions using your relationship and communication skills to improve the art of feedback and advice giving.

> Few people learn best by having information dumped into their brains.

FROM THE FRONTLINE

The heat is up in every sense of the word. It's a hot summer evening, with athletes sweating before they even take the field. Every player and coach is living with the knowledge that this is an important game, perhaps the most crucial game of the season. Everyone is tense, especially the team's head coach. He feels the pressure to win, and it's coming through as he beseeches the team to do this and remember that. The coach is particularly focused on a few talented players, all of whom have their heads buried, averting eye contact and seemingly waiting for the tirade to end.

A few questions arise from this scene:

- Why don't the players seem to respond too well to the advice being given?
- How much of this are they taking in, and how is it being received?
- Is there another way of going about this job?

Imparting information forcefully is a common phenomenon in coaching at all levels. We as coaches repeat messages over and over, often at higher volumes when they are not adhered to. MI presents another path in which you engage the team or individual athlete in the discussion about your plan, even in the most tense sports moments.

Imagine you are an athlete discussing your running race strategy with a coach and you have a choice between receiving one of these forms of advice. Which of the following would you prefer and why?

> "No, listen here: It's not like that; you want to move quicker, not slower, at that point in the race because they will catch you and then box you in. Can you see that?"

"I wonder about the potential of you moving quicker at that point in the race, to prevent them boxing you in. What do you think?"

One way to judge your reaction is to read the first one again and then stop and notice what your immediate reaction is. Is it as if someone is pushing you in one direction, and you want to kick back and think something like "Yes, but hang on a moment . . ."?

When we present this exercise to colleagues in sports, they overwhelmingly vote in favor of the second intervention, which goes along with comments like, "I don't mind getting clear advice, but I like to be part of the decision making"; or "I prefer not to be told what to do all the time." Advice giving can descend into coercion that people react against (see Chapter 1).

FROM THE FRONTLINE

So we made a pact. The coaches—myself included—agreed we would not speak to him about his method . . . no longer would he have support staff stopping him every second ball in the nets, telling him to change his grip, stance, backlift or alignment. Instead, the only advice would be when he sought it and based solely on his game plan for any given day. . . . Ultimately we have backed Jonny to take responsibility for his own game, and the results are there to see.

—Jason Gillespie, Yorkshire cricket coach (Gillespie, 2015)

How much training have you had on *how* to give advice and feedback to athletes? Few coaches report receiving support with this task, so one has to learn on the job and read the signals about the right time to give the advice, how much to give, what to say, and how to help athletes be motivated to act on it. Some coaches have a lot of experience in giving feedback. But we all know we can get better at it, to achieve coaching mastery. Like it or not, *how* you communicate information to an athlete could be as important as the actual advice or feedback you deliver. Among the questions we raise with coaches are: "How often do you emphasize choice when you give advice?" and "How curious are you about the athlete's uptake of the advice immediately afterward?"

TIP: *Develop curiosity about what athletes make of your advice or feedback.*

Before turning to the strategy itself, consider for a moment how and why advice can fall on deaf ears.

What Can Go Wrong?

COACH: No, listen here: It's not like that; you want to move quicker, not slower, at that point in the race because they will catch you and then box you in. Can you see that?

ATHLETE: OK. Thanks, Coach.

COACH: So what will you do next time?

ATHLETE: I don't know really; it depends on who I am racing against I guess.

COACH: Well, remember what I suggest, and see if you can give it a try.

ATHLETE: Yes. Thanks, Coach. (*Walks away thinking, "I doubt I can do that."*)

We've all been there. You feel strongly that you can see where things could improve, you offer feedback or advice, and you get that blank look in response. It might come with a nod, or a "thank you," but either way you don't really know how much of an impact your words have had. Persuading an athlete to change has its drawbacks, for you as well as for the athlete.

Why does this happen so often? Some of the answers probably sit in a traditional view that has the coach as the expert and the athlete as the passive recipient of the coach's advice, usually focused on deficits, things that are not right. It's then just one short step to see it as the coach's job to fill the vacuum, a bit like lifting the lid on a player's head, putting the advice inside, and then closing the lid and checking whether it has "sunk in." As we march on looking for deficits to correct, learning can get left behind. You probably notice moments when you or other coaches nail it as they give advice by really connecting with athletes, but what exactly does skillful practice look like, and how can you replicate it and improve your approach? The short answer we found in developing MI and the strategy below was to find a way of ensuring that the athlete is much more active in the advice-giving task. The strategy below has evolved from introducing MI into sports and working with coaches to distill the most efficient way to give advice. Rather than a whole new way of advice giving, it is more a method of sticking to the most effective parts of advice giving that you sometimes engage in.

STRATEGY: ASK–OFFER–ASK

Summary: Developed and refined in MI over 20 years, this strategy improves the uptake and effectiveness of advice and feedback. It involves listening before and after conveying key information. Box 10.1 summarizes the strategy.

In time, as you refine your practice and get more efficient with those listening statements, your conversations will become more smooth and free of needless words. This both saves you time and makes the time you do spend more valuable. The reaction of athletes becomes your guide for making judgments about whether to provide more information or leave it for a while. Again, nothing in this chapter is newly invented, and the skillful practice examples can be seen in the work of good coaches and teachers everywhere. What we present here is a strategy we have used in training people worldwide, in different settings and circumstances.

> Check in before *and*
> *after* you give advice.

The strategy itself is not a rigid sequence but simply a guide for moving between asking and offering. Not sure what someone already knows?

BOX 10.1. A Framework for Feedback and Advice

There is a simple structure that can make giving advice and feedback more effective. You start and end by asking athletes for their take on the information you provide.

Ask

"What do you already know or have tried?"
"What would you really like to know?"

Offer

Attempt to present your idea as an informed suggestion. Keep to facts if you can, and leave it to them to clarify their relevance. Stay positive (offering ideas about what to do rather than what not to do—"How about leaning forward?" rather than "Don't lean back"). Offer choices if you are giving advice. Use language like "might" rather than "should"; and "I wonder whether . . ." rather than "Something you must do is. . . ."

Ask

"What do you think of my suggestion?"
"How does my idea fit with your plan?"
"What will work the best or the worst here?"
"How could you improve given what we've talked about?"

Check it out and connect first. Do they want advice *now*? How might your feedback affect their practice? Ask them and listen. You might hear them say positive things about their hopes and plans for improving their performance, what we call change talk, which is when you can use MI to champion and reinforce these aspirations.

> **TIP:** *If you are not sure how the advice is landing, ask the athletes; they are your best resource.*

EXAMPLES

Giving Advice about Technique

Technical advice is best expressed only after you have developed a connection and good relationship with an athlete. Overdoing it, giving too much advice too soon, is a danger well known to coaches. One of the main shifts here for you is from being the deficit detective to being an expert champion of choice, and it's a state of mind in the first instance (see Chapter 2).

Ask Permission and Open Up the Conversation (Ask)

Asking permission is not a bad place to start—for example: "Is it OK if we talk for a few minutes about a couple of things?" (asking permission), or "How much would you like to look at changing your [technique or strategy]?" The idea is for you both to develop curiosity about improvement—for example: "How do you feel you are getting on with this [technique]?"; "What ideas do you have?" Athletes often hesitate at this point because it's easier to keep to what they know than venture into new territory. Trying something new is a risk that opens them up to negative results, possible embarrassment, and criticism.

Champion Freedom of Choice When You Offer Advice (Offer)

When you provide advice, offer a choice if possible, even if it's to take it or not: "There are some options for the next practice for you here—what can we focus on?"; "You seem to be slipping a bit with your left arm, and it might be better to think about doing it like this . . . [explain], or keep to what you are doing now." Your language is modest, not inflexible—for example: "It's up to you whether to act on this advice." It's the experience of freedom to choose that makes athletes most receptive to advice.

> **TIP:** *The more you respect the athletes' choice, the more likely they are to take your advice.*

Return to the Athlete for a Decision (Ask)

What do you notice in your athlete's body language and reaction? How does your athlete feel about your feedback or advice? Check it out by asking a question like "What do you think?" or "How might that work for you?" (ask). The listening you do at this point could be the key that unlocks athletes' courage to change, and you will be using MI as part of a very normal conversation. You will be lighting the fire within them.

> **TIP:** Listening after giving advice is often the key to unlocking athletes' courage to make the change. That's where the power of MI kicks in.

Use MI to Take the Conversation Forward

COACH: (*Gives the advice and then:*) What do you think? How might that work for you?

ATHLETE: I'm not sure; it's a big change, Coach.

COACH: You don't want to make a mistake here with this decision. [listening statement]

ATHLETE: Exactly. I guess I could try it [change talk] and always go back to my old ways if it doesn't work out.

COACH: That could be an important turning point, making that decision. [listening statement]

ATHLETE: Yeah, well, let's see how it goes—this new plan—and just don't disappear today if it doesn't work out. (*Laughs.*) [change talk]

A Feedback Discussion

A conversation where you give feedback, formal or not, is a good opportunity to lift athlete confidence and develop a "can-do" attitude. Essentially, you talk about data; the athletes talk about what it means for them. It's often really useful to raise their level of curiosity to begin with, starting off by asking a question like "What would you most like to get out of this feedback?" (ask). Then you stick to the observations or facts as closely as you can (offer), and then step back and use open questions about their meaning for the athlete (ask). For example: "Can we take a moment to look at your times over a period of a year? [Ask permission; wait for the athlete to nod or say yes.] What do you think we might see here? What interests you the most [ask]?"

The athlete responds for a minute or two. Then you present the performance data or your observations (offer). Notice the curious and nonconfrontational attitude behind the way a coach moves from offering to asking:

> "There's these times here, around December and January, that show a slowing down, and then they pick up [offer]. I've got a few ideas that I want to mention to you, but what do you make of this [ask]?"
> "When we look at this journal, I notice there could be a link between diet and your times. Look at this week here. There's a family gathering and a party, and it makes me wonder about what's going on [offer]? What do you think might be going on here [ask]?"
> "Some athletes get fatigued by overdoing it in practice; others find a balance. Here, just last month, your volume of practice is the highest. The effect on your competition times is worth noticing: They go down [offer], or maybe that's because of something else [ask]?"

In each of these short exchanges, there's mileage in pausing to reconnect, with questions like "What's going on here?" or "What's the take-home message for you?" (ask). The athlete will naturally start talking about change and how this might happen (change talk). MI thrives on this kind of conversation. The goal of feedback is as much to develop curiosity as it is to correct problems.

Use MI to Take the Conversation Forward

COACH: What do you make of this data and feedback about your volume of practice and the risk of overdoing it?

ATHLETE: Am I trying too hard? Is that what you are saying?

COACH: You're wondering if you're trying too hard. [listening statement]

ATHLETE: Well, who doesn't push themselves? It's what we are trained to do.

COACH: Yeah. It's not easy to know where the middle ground is, between slacking and overdoing it.

ATHLETE: That's me. I swing this way and that, and I need to get better at finding a balance. [change talk] You say my times are going down last month when my practice volume is highest?

COACH: Possibly. I wonder how we can get better at finding this balance? [open question about change; using MI to call for change talk]

ATHLETE: It's got to be about me understanding my body and trusting that, like when I feel it's not right, pushing myself a bit hard; maybe I should listen to that.

COACH: Some players check in with the training staff before practice to decide how much they should push themselves. What will work best for you?

Team Feedback

Team feedback usually develops a familiar routine, where players and coach go through what went wrong and right in a game, or consider strategy for an upcoming game. A guiding principle of MI is that giving feedback will work well when players feel free to talk about what they think and feel, and can safely give voice to how they can improve. For sure the coach will have feedback and advice to offer, but in the end it's how the players make use of information that will matter. A quiet room may signify respect, but it also may signify athletes' apprehensions about speaking up and serve as a sign that engagement just isn't there.

Most coaches stress accountability. That is, most think it is important for players to take responsibility for their actions on and off the field. Managers, coaches, or support staff can certainly hold players accountable; however, in MI we believe that athletes holding *themselves* accountable in a team setting is one of the most powerful team-building moments possible. How do we encourage that? How might the strategy in this chapter help to improve things in these group sessions? The ask–offer–ask strategy turns a potentially passive feedback session into something much more dynamic, in which you start by asking them how they feel their game went (ask), provide some of your observations (offer), and then ask them what sense they make of your input (ask). The ground rules for group discussion will be important too: Should they be discouraged from blaming others and rather just speak about themselves? How do you keep things positive? What structure for discussion will lift the energy in the room and help them to head out with motivation high? Questions like these are addressed in Chapters 11 and 12 on teamwork.

> Feedback develops curiosity as well as corrects problems.

CONCLUSION

Giving advice, talking about technique, and offering feedback can be done briefly without losing the spirit or essence of this ask–offer–ask framework. It's about not just transmitting your knowledge but also framing the discussion within your positive relationship, and the mindset of a guide, to provide challenges and new ideas that give athletes the courage to experiment, a strategy that you can practice at every turn.

QUESTIONS TO CONSIDER

■ How easy will it be, before giving feedback to athletes, to ask them what they think?

■ What am I doing to help the other coaches avoid using the righting reflex too much?

■ When giving advice or feedback, do you talk most of the time?

PART III

AROUND THE FIELD

We suspect you will agree that you want athletes to be driven not by a fear of failure or punishment, but by coaching that helps them to enjoy and express themselves, as individuals and with others. Their confidence, willingness to listen, and freedom from fear will be more important than conformity.

Around the field of play is where relationships get built that help you achieve these goals. It's in those conversations with parents and informal exchanges with colleagues and athletes that the use of MI can help, not just to build confidence in athletes, but also to develop a culture in a team or club that is much bigger than the sum of its parts, a place where people thrive.

That's the theory, so to speak, that introduces Part III. Now to the practice:

Teamwork and how to use MI to promote it is covered within the opening chapters of Part III. Chapter 11 covers the first step: Develop teamwork by improving the social skills of athletes to say what they think and feel. Then the second step is built on this foundation: Help athletes to work on the ultimate teamwork task, which is making decisions together (Chapter 12). Stronger bonds will make for better decisions of all kinds, including results in competition.

Athlete behavior change, well-being, and lifestyle is the subject of Chapter 13, which presents three MI strategies that can be used to make solid progress when you talk about these topics with athletes. Health and well-being are home territory for MI, which was developed specifically for this purpose. Athletes who experience balance in their lives more broadly will perform better and contribute much to team morale.

Coaching in poor communities (Chapter 14) addresses the use of MI either by coaches working in poor communities or with athletes that have a background of hardship or deprivation. It is cowritten with Rob Maitra, a trainer in MI and schoolteacher who has many years of experience engaging with young people who bring the weight of disadvantage into their sporting lives.

From connecting well to culture change is the subject of the final chapter, in which we look at how improved communication can form the foundation of better outcomes and culture change in sports. We use the example of a baseball club's phenomenal rise to the top, driven by the passion of all involved to work in an atmosphere of respect, trust, and open communication—the ideal home for MI.

CHAPTER 11

Teamwork 1

DEVELOPING SOCIAL SKILLS

> To me, teamwork is the beauty of our sport, where you
> have five acting as one. You become selfless.
> —MIKE KRZYZEWSKI, baseball coach

HIGHLIGHTS

+ Better relationships mean better teamwork.
+ Help athletes with the social skill of saying what they think
  and feel—it's a direct route to improving trust, respect, and
  teamwork.
+ Use MI skills (questions, listening statements, and
  summaries) in open discussion to promote this social skill.
  Guidelines and illustrations are provided in this chapter.
+ The next chapter moves up a step with guidelines for making
  decisions together.

This chapter and the one that follows present a two-step sequence
for using MI to improve teamwork: first, helping athletes to develop their
social skills and express themselves in a group (Step 1 in this chapter) and
then, second, using this skill to make decisions together (Step 2 in the next
chapter).

THE KICKOFF

If MI can be used with individual athletes, what about in teams, where
you encourage players to bond and build cohesion? Can you use MI skills

and that mindset of a guide to help them say what they want and need, just as you might with an individual, and commit to action, united? In other words, can MI be used to improve teamwork?

It's called the holy grail of sports—how to develop teamwork—and it continues to puzzle coaches, analysts, and even scientists. It's difficult to define, a bit like love, something that happens between people that is positive and powerful. Developing it is another matter. You might *want* a group of athletes to commit to the common cause, but you can't force them to be united because what matters sits in their hearts and they must feel that commitment and be willing to act on it. Accessing the hearts of people can be a challenge.

Yet teams clearly do rise up and achieve remarkable things. Most sportspeople know that feeling of being "selfless," as Krzyzewski says in the quote that opens this chapter, of working together in an openhearted way that lifts willpower and performance, and where the whole is greater than the sum of its parts. As one commentator put it, "Understanding [the] chemistry [of teamwork] is an interesting philosophical problem; creating it is a practical one" (Rowen, 2018).

FROM THE FRONTLINE

Trouble broke out when a college football player had an argument with a teacher at school, got disciplined, and was then roundly punished by the head coach of the club. The coach decided to punish the whole squad, "to teach them all a lesson." They were obliged to run around the field five times. One of them vomited; another had an asthma attack. This was tough to watch for our coach friend. She was lower in status to the head coach. It was not her way of doing things; she did not believe that punishment and fear induction were the best routes to improvement, and she was concerned about the effect of this punishment on team morale. She needn't have been. The team captain asked her not to enter the locker room so they could sort out the trouble themselves. They did just that, said what they felt about the episode, helped their "offending" teammate to feel supported rather than blamed, and agreed on a plan of action that included one letter to the school from the athlete and one to the head coach from the whole team. They walked out of the locker room with their heads held high.

Young people generally learn fast—and in this team, over a period of about a year, they had learned to trust each other, say what they feel, and make decisions together. Then they were able to move forward, united. They knew how to do this because their coach, our friend, had trusted them and helped them over that year to develop these social and problem-solving skills in the first place.

Two Key Tasks

Two standout coaching tasks emerge from the above story and they provide the framework for the next two chapters, both involving the use of MI in a group:

- Step 1: Help athletes to develop social skills, to say what they think and feel in a group and to listen to each other (this chapter).
- Step 2: Help them to make decisions as a unit (Chapter 12).

Each of these tasks can be worked on using MI with athletes in small and large groups. The more they develop the relevant skills, the more they will feel comfortable in their own skin, even share their vulnerabilities, and the easier it will be for them to make decisions together, as a unit. We start in this chapter with social skills, Step 1 above: "Express yourself with fellow athletes." In the next chapter we turn to using MI to help athletes harness their skills to make decisions together.

> The more comfortable they feel, the easier it will be to make decisions together.

WHAT SOCIAL SKILLS?

Legendary teams are worth studying—they seem to exhibit high levels of social skills. The 2016 Chicago Cubs squad is a good example, and in journalist Tom Verducci's account of their winning the World Series, there is a standout message: They worked on and improved social skills and relationships first. Indeed, when asked about the principles that guided the journey of the subsequently successful team, coach Joe Madden was able to list them. Number 1 on the list was this: "Make a personal connection first: Everything else follows" (Verducci, 2017, p. 190).

Working with and through relationship-building using MI is a direct route to improving social skills and developing teamwork; the key athlete skills are listed in Box 11.1.

It's not difficult to see why very skilled and successful coaches talk about the importance of humility and the need to model the social skills yourself, listen to others, be prepared to get it wrong and admit this, and convey respect for others as people. Next up is probably patience and tolerance because you can't make people what they are not. With their different personalities and backgrounds, some players will be keener than others to develop their social skills. Acceptance of difference is a social skill in itself.

BOX 11.1. Key Social Skill Targets for MI in Groups of Athletes

- Say what you think and how you feel, free of fear.
- Learn to listen to others.
- Avoid blaming others unnecessarily.
- Respect each other as people first, athletes second.
- Interrupt less.
- Allow quieter fellow athletes to have their voices heard.

FROM THE FRONTLINE

In an elite rugby club, one that was right up there with the best in the world, we came across bottle openers spread around the recreational space that all had a set of identical questions engraved on them: "What's your favorite hobby?" "What's the most frightening recent experience you can remember?" "Who is your favorite rugby player and why?" When asked what these were used for, the coach said that in strategy meetings the plan was always to start with an open discussion prompted by a question or two from the bottle opener, to encourage the team to express themselves. Then they moved on to game strategy.

To develop these social skills in a team, the topic you choose for open discussion does not really matter, as long as athletes are interested in it. It might be directly linked to their sport, or be more personal. It might be set up a bit formally as in the example above, or it might be right in the middle of a hectic strategy discussion. Every time you talk with them, whether with two athletes while you walk to practice or in a large and more formal team meeting, they have the opportunity to express themselves and you have the opportunity to model good practice and use the MI skills outlined in this chapter. The phrase "every conversation counts" is clearly relevant here. Athletes who can express themselves are better able to think, process, and form good relationships with others. Upon this foundation they can make decisions together and seal the bonds that make for lasting teamwork.

STRATEGY: HELP THEM SAY WHAT THEY THINK AND FEEL

Summary: Provide guidelines that help players to feel safe, and then use MI skills to promote open discussion.

The Strategy in Action

Imagine a balloon being tossed by the coach into the group, starting with an open question for them to discuss. The balloon is the conversation, and the goal is for them to toss the balloon around among themselves, with the coach occasionally intervening to help keep going.

In the example below, the coach wants team members to talk about their best ways to prepare for an upcoming match.

> COACH: Everyone is different. What's the best way for you to prepare for a really important upcoming match when you wake up in the morning?
>
> ATHLETE A: I try not to think about it until I get to the field; that's the best way to stay calm.
>
> ATHLETE B: No, that's hopeless because it's like you are shutting it all out. I get these butterflies in my stomach on match day, and I can't ignore them.
>
> ATHLETE A: Ah . . . hey, but you don't want to get too nervous too soon.
>
> COACH: What do some of the others think? [encouraging discussion]
>
> ATHLETE C: I get very focused into match zone and pack my kit bag full of the most important things in the world. I clean my boots way more than I need to, but that gets me right into the zone.
>
> ATHLETE B: I do need to calm down a bit, so I listen to music while I eat breakfast, nice and calm before the storm.
>
> ATHLETE D: You guys are bonkers. (*Laughs.*) . . . Just get to the damn ground and get on with it, you bunch of losers.
>
> ATHLETE A: Exactly. You guys think about it too much.
>
> COACH: Has anyone heard anything that sounds useful to them?
>
> ATHLETE B: I reckon I am sloppy with packing my kit bag, so that sounds like a useful idea, to do this in a nice, focused way.
>
> COACH: Let's move on to the game today. Anyone like to suggest what our most important task will be?
>
> ATHLETE E: Keeping ourselves tight as a unit, very, very tight.
>
> COACH: That feels important to you.
>
> ATHLETE F: We know about keeping tight and together, but I wonder about being a bit more aggressive today and taking a few risks?

Replay the Tape

That took a minute or two, and the coach had an easy time of it because those athletes seem happy to say what they think and feel. They tossed the balloon around quite easily.

Statement	What's going on?
COACH: Everyone is different. What's the best way for you to prepare for a really important upcoming match when you wake up in the morning?	*Open question encourages open discussion.*
ATHLETE A: I try not to think about it until I get to the field; that's the best way to stay calm.	
ATHLETE B: No, that's hopeless because it's like you are shutting it all out. I get these butterflies in my stomach on match day, and I can't ignore them.	*Cuts across a fellow athlete and produces her own idea; coach decides to not intervene.*
ATHLETE A: Ah . . . hey, but you don't want to get too nervous too soon.	
COACH: What do some of the others think?	*Coach offers another question to encourage discussion.*
ATHLETE C: I get very focused into match zone and pack my kit bag full of the most important things in the world. I clean my boots way more than I need to, but that gets me right into the zone.	*Even expresses vulnerability: " . . . way more than I need to."*
ATHLETE B: I do need to calm down a bit, so I listen to music while I eat breakfast, nice and calm before the storm.	
ATHLETE D: You guys are bonkers. (*Laughs.*) . . . Just get to the damn ground and get on with it, you bunch of losers.	*Jokes with an affectionate tone—builds unity.*
ATHLETE A: Exactly. You guys think about it too much.	*Encouraging others to reflect.*

Statement	What's going on?
COACH: Has anyone heard anything that sounds useful to them?	*Open question that calls for change talk.*
ATHLETE B: I reckon I am sloppy with packing my kit bag, so that sounds like a useful idea, to do this in a nice, focused way.	*Change talk emerges.*
COACH: Let's move on to the game today. Anyone like to suggest what our most important task will be?	*Coach shifts focus.*
ATHLETE E: Keeping ourselves tight as a unit, very, very tight.	*Change talk.*
COACH: That feels important to you.	*Simple listening statement that reinforces change talk and invites this athlete or others to contribute.*
ATHLETE F: We know about keeping tight and together, but I wonder about being a bit more aggressive today and taking a few risks?	*Change talk.*

The coach started with an open discussion that warmed up the athletes for talking about the day's game strategy. If some of the best moves in sports are simple and free of complications, so it is with group facilitation— keeping to basics is what this coach did, or put another way, it's useful to note what she *didn't* do. She never took over the discussion or passed judgment. She used a couple of open questions and then sat back and let them toss the balloon around. She tolerated their different views—in fact, she enjoyed letting them express themselves. She also had the skill to use a listening statement right at the end ("That feels important to you"), the aim of which was not to answer her own question but to toss the balloon back to them in the hope that someone else might open up, which happened. The best way to teach social skills is not to teach social skills but to get out of the way while they do this for themselves.

You might be wondering something like "That's such an easy topic to talk about, preparing for a match, but what happens when it's serious stuff, when the players are upset and start disagreeing with each other?" The logic we are using is that if they get used to saying what they think and feel with easy topics, they will be better placed when the going gets tough, a subject we address later in this chapter. Balloons do pop in group discussion. It's the coach's job to toss another one into the space for them to try again.

Getting It Right

Open discussion is not naturally or necessarily constructive, which is why you need to provide some clear guidelines so athletes know what is useful and acceptable, and what is off limits. We noticed one coach asking a squad of athletes to decide about these ground rules themselves and saw them bond in front of our eyes as they agreed about what was and was not acceptable; more likely in the future, this team will follow their own established "rules." Coaches can be concerned that by allowing a team to decide their own rules, they may invite a lack of discipline. Encouraging a team to initiate their own rules doesn't prohibit a coach from modifying the rules at any point. Box 11.2 provides an overview of principles and practice.

> Athletes set ground rules.

After reminding athletes about the guidelines, you then move into a state in which you might feel uncomfortable not to be in control of the discussion. Yet letting go of this control is important if you want them to develop the social habits of talking and listening. You can remind yourself that you are choosing to give the athletes control temporarily and that you can regain control whenever you want to. A lightness of touch also helps because when people laugh, they lower their defenses and are more open to learn. Over time, your use of open discussion helps to develop a culture of mutual trust in the team, with a more even power balance—one of the foundations of teamwork—where players feel increasingly safe and willing to express their vulnerabilities.

> When people laugh, they learn.

FROM THE FRONTLINE

Each of the authors has had this challenge many times in open discussion: The answers that come back are way off what we were hoping for. At first, the fear that this might happen put us off open discussion altogether. Then we learned how to take back control when we heard too many athlete offerings that were off center. We summarize, without passing judgment or countering what they have said, and then we simply redirect the discussion and guide them with another open question to see if they can be more constructive. If all else fails, we jump in and fix the problem.

> ## BOX 11.2. Open Discussion: Getting It Right
>
> ### Guidelines
>
> - Respect for each other is an important value.
> - Speak for yourself and about how you feel, rather than about others.
> - Listen rather than interrupt.
> - Feel free to say nothing.
> - Give space to the quieter ones to speak as well.
> - We are in this as a team, together.
>
> ### MI Skills
>
> - Clear, open questions.
> - Listening statements.
> - Summaries.
>
> ### Coach Conduct
>
> - Remind them about guidelines.
> - Ask a positive, open question about something they have in common.
> - Avoid interrupting, passing judgment, or solving problems.
> - Use listening statements. Capture what's been said, and hand it straight back to them to say more.
> - If all goes quiet, consider questions like "What else?" or "What do others think/feel?"
> - Summarize before moving on.

We often spend 20% of the total meeting time in open discussion, usually splitting this time between the beginning and end of the meeting. Will some athletes roll their eyes feeling that this kind of question is just about "fluff"? They might, especially when they first experience the process, but your task is to show them you mean business and act accordingly. They won't think it's fluff when you ask them to address a really serious problem.

A point might come in the discussion when it's your turn to summarize. You might note this or that problem, but your main task is to highlight things said that they have in common, and offer this back to them, like handing out gifts. For example, you have a team meeting just before a practice session. You started the meeting with a question like "What's your main priority for the practice today?" After 5 minutes of open discussion, you might summarize: "You are maybe not sure about *a* and *b*, but you have some smart ideas about how to enjoy this session today and work together as a group." The cycle looks a bit like this: You ask, they say, you make a listening statement, they say some more, and then you highlight the key points in a summary. Teamwork and bonding will improve as a result.

TO THE NEXT LEVEL: CLEARING THE AIR

Once you and the athletes are comfortable with the basics of talking in a group, you can move to the next level, where you build teamwork by diving into tough and sensitive topics, coming out on the other side stronger and more united. For example, some athletes might be really cross about being left out of a team, and you can see little groups forming that split the squad and create disunity; perhaps you notice that while the team is in a bit of a downward spiral, the players seem to be doing nothing but complaining and blaming others; or perhaps out there around the field of play, things are going a bit out of control. It's time to clear the air, and MI skills can help you do this.

FROM THE FRONTLINE

The sport was cricket, but so common is this scenario that you might wonder why coaches are not given special training in managing group conflict. The team was doing badly, the stakes were high, and sparks were flying in and around them, including in the media. It was what they call "The Ashes," a hotly contested series of matches between Australia and England. What went wrong on that 2013–14 tour has been keenly dissected. The team were losing match after match; players were not united on the field; the locker room was not a happy place; a key player suffered a stress reaction and went home; another retired for good at short notice. Inside accounts reveal that a key meeting to clear the air was not constructive. Open disagreement between players and coaches were not resolved. Some felt that they were not being honest with each other.

—Tom Fordyce (2017), sports writer

Clearing the air in group discussion to address "hot" issues involves having faith in both yourself and others, and having the group management skills to see it through to a constructive resolution. Sometimes it seems that all involved dance around the issue, having everything but the conversation that really matters.

One MI strategy guideline we use is to start by helping athletes to say what they think and feel by using a following style (see Box 11.2 on p. 149); then you take more control, switching to a guiding style, and ask them a few choice open questions designed to pull constructive answers from them—for example: "How do you guys want to end this meeting?"; "How do you see the best way forward?"; "What can you offer to the group that can be helpful?"; and "What help do you need from others to make things better?" These are simple guiding questions, and the answers to them can profoundly improve teamwork. Finally, you might model good leadership and use a fixing style to say exactly how you would like them to proceed. Notice how this approach to managing problems in a group mirrors precisely the "follow–guide–fix" strategy presented in Chapter 8 for addressing behavior problems with individual athletes (see Figure 8.1 on p. 95).

THE POWER OF CONNECTION

It's through these relationship-building conversations that legendary teams rise to tell stories about how they had a special bond that made all the difference. Coaches must have helped them to build their relationships over time so they could make sharp collective decisions as a unit. MI can be used as a potentially powerful aid to improve relationships, whether in a meeting, on the side of a field, or after a competition or game. Every little success will make a difference to team unity and increase the chances of succeeding at whatever plans they make.

QUESTIONS TO CONSIDER

- How much freedom do your athletes feel to speak their minds?
- Imagine yourself sitting in a group meeting and providing guidelines for the discussion as in Box 11.2.
- When athletes form cliques and leave others feeling less important to their peers, what can you do about this? Should you do anything about it?

CHAPTER 12

Teamwork 2

MAKING DECISIONS AS A UNIT

> I always tell my players to find the fire within themselves.
> —CLAUDIO RANIERI, soccer coach

HIGHLIGHTS

+ Use MI skills to help a team make decisions together.
+ Start with easier decisions first, to help athletes get used to the idea.
+ Use open questions and listening statements to invite them to reach agreement.
+ Use small groups and a "one-at-a-time" method for maximum efficiency.

Chapter 11 covered Step 1 for using MI to improve teamwork: helping athletes to develop social skills, to say what they think and feel in front of each other. This chapter covers Step 2: helping them to use this social skill to make decisions together.

THE KICKOFF

Athletes with the skill and the willingness to express themselves in their group will find it easier and more enjoyable to work as a team. That was the focus of the last chapter. Now what? There's a second step to building teamwork in which athletes make decisions together, a powerful force for bonding and lifting motivation in which they put their own egos to one side for the common good. This is not a quick, magic route to building teamwork but a task that they get better at over time. While other routes, such as the inspiring team talk from a coach, are more widely used, this one follows the logic of MI, that inspiration and motivation is most powerful when it comes from within.

FROM THE FRONTLINE

Carlo Ancelotti is a highly respected and successful elite soccer coach. He was facing a crucial season-defining game, the last of the season, when he announced, "This is the last game of the season. We know what we're able to do and we know the opposition. What do you think the tactics should be?"

One of his fellow coaches, Paul Clement takes up the story:

Carlo's question silenced a group of players not renowned for being shy. They weren't used to being asked for their thoughts. Their ideas. But, gradually, baffled expressions turned into ones of contemplation. And then the hands went up.

I started writing. [Three well-known players] made key contributions that night. And as the others warmed to the idea, more got involved. I scribbled notes down as fast as I could and, before you knew it, we had a list of defending points and a list of attacking ones.

That was it. The tactics were decided, the team talk was done and the next day the players went on and delivered. A 1–0 victory. A historic [victory]. A player-led approach. (Clement, 2017)

With the strategy below in your toolbox, you can practice using a wide range of techniques for helping athletes make decisions together. We turn first to the strategy itself, its guiding principles and inner workings, and then to examples of how it can be used in different circumstances.

STRATEGY: MAKING DECISIONS TOGETHER

Summary: Use a guiding style to help athletes say what they think and feel about a decision to be made, and support them to reach agreement.

It's an act of faith, helping them to make decisions together, when you decide that they have the inspiration and wisdom inside them to find a solution.

The Strategy in Action

It's an ice hockey team. The challenge is a near universal one: cell phones invading the time to focus on the game. Can the coach help them to make a decision for themselves?

COACH: The coaching team have decided that we must do something to reduce the use of cell phones in and around the locker room because these are times when we want you to be together as a group, whether having a laugh or talking more seriously about the game. It improves togetherness. We don't want to make the decision for you, but we invite you to work together now to decide on exactly what the guidelines should be.

ATHLETE A: I knew that was coming because Coach Smith caught Carlos on his phone during that briefing last week.

COACH: So, there are times when it causes a little conflict, and you noticed that.

ATHLETE A: Why do we all have to suffer just because of Carlos?

ATHLETE B: Hold it—it's not just Carlos; all of us use our phones many times a day.

ATHLETE C: Well, I think we should do something, but I don't know what. I just like the idea of us making the decision together; then we all stick to it.

COACH: So, you guys have different views about this.

ATHLETE E: Well, I think Carlos should take some responsibility here; why should we all suffer?

ATHLETE A: I agree. I tell you, Carlos, I like you as a teammate, but that was over the top.

ATHLETE F (CARLOS): Well, I said sorry to you all, and that's that.

ATHLETE G: I accept your apology, Carlos, so let's get on with it.

COACH: I wonder what your best decision might be?

ATHLETE B: We got to do something guys, so let's get on with it.

ATHLETE A: OK, then let's just chill with the phones before practice.

COACH: You guys sound committed to moving forward now.

Replay the Tape

Statement	What's going on?
COACH: We don't want to make the decision for you, but we invite you to work together now to decide on exactly what the guidelines should be.	*Clear question for them. Conveys belief that they can and will solve the problem.*

Statement	What's going on?
ATHLETE A: I knew that was coming because Coach Smith caught Carlos on his phone during that briefing last week.	*Signal of resistance—blaming someone else. Important to use the rolling with resistance strategy (see Chapter 6).*
COACH: So, there are times when it causes a little conflict, and you noticed that.	*Listening statement that rolls with the resistance and even affirms the athlete's powers of observation.*
ATHLETE A: Why do we all have to suffer just because of Carlos?	*Athlete A continues to blame Carlos.*
ATHLETE B: Hold it—it's not just Carlos; all of us use our phones many times a day.	*Expresses his feelings, free of fear (see Chapter 11).*
ATHLETE C: Well, I think we should do something, but I don't know what. I just like the idea of us making the decision together; then we all stick to it.	*Change talk.*
COACH: So, you guys have different views about this.	*Simple listening statement that captures the mood of the group as a whole; no pressure from the coach, who trusts them to provide their own pressure to make a decision. The statement also invites them to express their views, which the next athlete readily takes up.*
ATHLETE E: Well, I think Carlos should take some responsibility here; why should we all suffer?	*Another effort to blame Carlos.*
ATHLETE A: I agree. I tell you Carlos, I like you as a teammate, but that was over the top.	*More blaming.*
ATHLETE F (CARLOS): Well, I said sorry to you all, and that's that.	*Open, honest reply.*
ATHLETE G: I accept your apology, Carlos, so let's get on with it.	*Respectful. Change talk.*
COACH: I wonder what your best decision might be?	*Coach nudges them toward decision making with a pointed, open guiding question about change.*

Statement	What's going on?
ATHLETE B: We got to do something guys, so let's get on with it.	*Change talk.*
ATHLETE A: OK, then let's just chill with the phones before practice.	*He comes around to the emerging consensus; backs down; expresses change talk.*
COACH: You guys sound committed to moving forward now.	*Coach uses listening statement to highlight change talk.*

The temptation here is to fix. To tell the athletes what is required of them and why. However, this coach resisted the righting reflex and used all the best elements of MI, such as faith in their good judgment, curiosity about their motivations, and awareness about *not* jumping in to solve the problem for them. His use of open questions and listening statements were invitations for them to bond as a group and move forward toward a decision. He tossed these invitations into the group like a balloon for them to bat around among themselves, aware of the need not to fall into the trap of having individual conversations between himself and any player. It was their conversation to have. Change talk, that signal of success with MI, emerged. It took just a few minutes.

> Open questions and listening statements are invitations.

Getting It Right

Building unity in decision making means being very focused and purposeful, with a clear goal in mind. If in an open discussion (see Chapter 11) you use a following style to help them speak up, in team decision making you use a guiding style and MI to help them reach agreement, while you take time to learn about what makes the athletes tick and notice why and when you might need to step in to refine any decisions that are being made. They pass that balloon around with a purpose. Box 12.1 summarizes what's involved.

Quality team decision making can be enhanced by MI skills and the associated mindset. Imagine the language used in answer to a question like "How will we work best to prepare for this competition?" It encourages answers from the group that are positive, what we call change talk. Then, just as in conversations with individuals, you call for more, encouraging it, linking one offering with another, and summarizing the best bits before you move on and add your own ideas to the mix.

> **BOX 12.1. Group Decision Making:**
> **Getting It Right**
>
> ## Guidelines
>
> Same as for open discussion (see Chapter 11): Respect, speak for yourself, listen to others without interrupting, feel free to say nothing
>
> ## MI Coaching Skills
>
> - Open questions that focus on improvement and a decision that needs to be made
> - Listening statements that focus on positive change talk
> - Summaries
>
> ## Coach Conduct
>
> - Remind them about guidelines, and trust their wisdom.
> - Ask a positive, forward-looking question about a decision.
> - Avoid interrupting, passing judgment, or solving problems.
> - Use listening statements to remark on positive things being said that aid decision making and hand the discussion back to athletes to say more and refine the decision.
> - If all goes quiet, consider questions like "What else?"; "What do others feel?"; or "How are we going to resolve this?"
> - Offer your own solutions as needed.
> - Summarize before moving on.

For Younger Athletes?

You might be tempted to conclude that guiding a group like this is just for older athletes, until you realize that younger athletes are usually much more curious than older ones. They are usually more flexible and adaptable. As they grapple with learning to get on well with others, using MI in the group is a powerful vehicle for social development. The questions you ask will need to be adjusted to their age and developmental level, but the process with them could be even easier than with older athletes. A question like "How will we work best to prepare for this competition?" among older athletes can be adapted for younger children by breaking things down into a series of simpler questions—for example: "What skill do you guys think we need to work on most?" and then "Great ideas! Out of X, Y, and Z, what is most important to practice before the competition this week?" You are then free to say something like "OK, great. We will start with Y, then move to Z and X if we have time. Great competition plan, team—let's go!" This method also leaves room at the end to add other suggestions you have if there has been something critical that was left out.

WHEN THE SEA GETS ROUGH

How often do you hear about teamwork going out of the window because athletes are in conflict with each other or a coach is in conflict with rebellious athletes, colleagues, or management? It can get toxic when there's a lot at stake, such as losing games, pride, money, or all three. We often hear the phrase "winning solves most problems." The opposite could be said of losing. Under threat, people react or withdraw, things can get worse, and the fallout can be damaging.

How often do you hear of teams and coaches reconciling and resolving conflict in a mature and constructive way? Do those working at all levels of sports have the skills to do this? How can MI help? Is there some way in which conflict can be seen as not a destructive thing but an opportunity to learn and move forward? Let's have a look inside a difficult group meeting to see how this might come about through using MI. (Chapter 6 on rolling with resistance covers this topic in more detail.)

"You have no right to accuse me of not trying. That's a lie!" A player shouts this in the middle of your postgame review and analysis with the team in the locker room. You had just raised the example of a delay in regrouping on the field, right after a fast break, and this player took your comments as a criticism. Around moments like this, a meeting can spiral downward or toward resolution.

> ATHLETE: You have no right to accuse me of not trying. That's a lie!
>
> COACH: Putting it all on you feels unfair. [uses a listening statement to "roll with resistance"]
>
> ATHLETE: Yeah, it does. We sucked out there today . . . some of us worse than others.
>
> COACH: It's tough to not play at our best, and tougher still to face that as a team. [listening statement]
>
> ATHLETE: @#$%! We aren't winning. This strategy isn't helping us.
>
> COACH: It's hard for you to see it working. [another listening statement]

ATHLETE: Yeah, OK, I'm sorry to get so amped. It's just so . . . I just want us to play better. [Athlete feels understood, steps back from argument, and even responds with change talk—"I just want us to play better."]

COACH: You're figuring out what adjustments we all need to make. How do others feel about what happened?

Notice how each listening statement from the coach involves acknowledging or coming alongside the athlete, to some degree. This helps her feel heard and calm down. "Rolling with resistance" in this way takes courage because you are not taking charge and fixing anything but throwing the ball back with an invitation to clarify. By doing this you are demonstrating respect for players' ability to behave more respectfully to each other and you. You will be enhancing teamwork, not eroding it.

To avoid unhelpful discussion, keep these key guidelines in mind:

- The most efficient way to help people calm down is to listen to them.
- Be respectful toward *people,* even if you remain hard on the *problem.*
- Stay as calm and as loose as possible (see Chapter 2 on mindset).
- Don't fight back; argue with logic. Confronting resistance usually leads to shutdown, or worse (see Chapter 6).
- Try to see through the athlete's aggravating words to the person struggling to be heard.
- Consider apologizing for aggravation, even if you remain committed to addressing a problem.

EXAMPLES OF TEAM DECISION MAKING

The examples below are all true, with identities of the participants protected, and they highlight the skillful way in which coaches have used MI to guide athletes to express themselves and make decisions together. Some involve using the whole group, while others involve small groups or the "one-at-a-time" method (see Box 12.2). In all cases they are on the lookout for positive change talk from the athletes, which they ask for, reinforce, and encourage. Summaries are particularly useful for gathering the change talk that has emerged. This has the effect of cementing unity and promoting rapid decision making.

Athletes Deciding about Team Rules

Nagging athletes is a bore, a chore, and often ineffective. Among the most common nags is tidying up after practice. Instead of making the decisions yourself, MI can be used to encourage this type of teamwork. Athletes will be more likely to keep to an agreement they themselves have made. Here are three simple steps for doing this:

1. Gather the group. Explain the task and raise the question ("What should we do about tidying up after practice?").
2. Let them have an *open discussion*—express how they feel about this (see Step 1 in Chapter 11).
3. Encourage them to make a *group decision* (Step 2).

This is team building from the inside. To begin with, it might be a seemingly chaotic free-for-all as they learn to listen to each other in a group, and as you learn to help them toss solutions around without taking over too soon. Their struggle will help them to learn social skills. You might step in at some point and help them resolve an issue. Your options might include summarizing the ideas that have come up, calling for a vote on a couple of options, or even making the decision yourself. Whatever you do, they have worked together as a team. As they listen and learn, they end up solving problems for themselves. We once overheard two high school basketball players asking a third how they could help her get to practice on time more often. That's teamwork, and it can be learned.

Learning from Conflict: A Fight Breaks Out

When something out of order like a fight or conflict between teammates happens, exerting authority and using punishment is usually a mixed blessing. Order might be re-established but perpetrators lose face and don't necessarily learn their lessons. Jenny is a softball coach in a poor community who used a guiding style to move out of a punishment mindset into one where she looked for and found a way to help fighting kids learn from the experience. Her approach has relevance for all levels of sports. Here's what she did.

One of the players in the group of 16- to 17-year-olds asked another player to stop swinging his arms as they gathered at the end of practice. He didn't, and by accident his arm made contact with her head; she thought it was deliberate, and the resulting fight had to be broken up by adults. Jenny asked another coach to take the two players aside and answer two questions: "What happened?" and "How can we repair the damage?" At the same time, Jenny gathered the whole squad together and encouraged them to answer the same questions, one by one, with everyone's arms outstretched on their teammates' shoulders. Because that second question was focused on change and what to do about something, what she heard in reply was change talk (see Chapter 3), and when she noticed this, she decided "to put [her] MI hat on and focus on making listening statements in reply to their suggestions." The ideas rolled out of the group, and they decided to ask both teammates to rejoin the group immediately and to give them the following message: "Whether it was an accident or not, we are a team so we stick together."

After the session her fellow coach told Jenny that the two fighters had agreed to write her a letter of apology. The wider squad had been able to both express themselves (Step 1) and make a decision together (Step 2). Teamwork was improved. The two fighters saved face and learned something about how to resolve conflict with their peers.

> Let the ideas roll out of the group.

Reviewing a Game Using the Ask—Offer—Ask Strategy

Here's a common scenario: you have an upcoming competition and around 30 minutes to review the plan before practice, and you want them to have a big say in developing the strategy. How can you help them walk away clear and united, with a feeling they own and will live up to the decisions they contributed to? The coach described in the next paragraph used the ask–offer–ask strategy to achieve this, an MI strategy that encourages answers and decisions from the athletes themselves (see Chapter 10).

The coach opened the session with a reminder about team values, that is, an equal voice for everyone, respect for each other, and the importance of coming up with ideas they can all commit to (see Box 11.2). His key question to them was "What's the best thing we can take into our big day on Saturday?" Notice how, having asked this good guiding question, he keeps using listening statements designed to help the team explore answers to his question.

CoACH: I ask again, what's the best thing we can take into our big day on Saturday? [a wide-open question to warm them up and start discussing how they want to improve; will elicit change talk]

ATHLETE 1: Intensity, I say. [change talk]

ATHLETE 2: I liked that look we had last time, when we all had that focus and we knew it, and we used the focus to recover possession as quickly as possible. [using affirmation with fellow athletes]

ATHLETE 3: I don't know, but I think we have got to really support each other, every time, whether we have got the ball or not. [change talk]

COACH: United, you say, with a look like you mean business. [listening statement]

ATHLETE 4 (THE CAPTAIN): And we got to be clear about the team we are up against. We need that today, Coach. [change talk]

ATHLETE 2: Yeah, I agree. What's the strategy, Boss?

COACH: We will get onto strategy in a moment, but I wonder what you mean by intensity; what is that for you?

ATHLETE 1: For me, it's getting into a relaxed groove when I'm ready for anything, really ready.

ATHLETE 3: Intensity for me means us working as a single unit.

ATHLETE 4: Come on guys; we're going to hang in there together, relaxed with focus, yes? (*Turns to group with a raised fist.*) [change talk]

ATHLETES IN UNISON: Yeah, yes, sir.

COACH: You want to be focused, and you want a clear strategy.

ATHLETES IN UNISON: Yeah, sir. (*laughter*).

That took just a minute or two. The coach let them take the lead and keep that balloon up in the air, then produced a single observation, a listening statement, that linked everything that had been said: "You want to be focused, and you want a clear strategy."

Then he shifted direction. It was time for them to clarify the strategy itself, and he used the ask–offer–ask framework to do this. He first connected by asking them what strategy made sense to them, gathering up their offerings, and tossing them back to them as if with the gentle tap of a balloon—no judgment, no cutting across them with his own ideas (ask). Less said, faster progress. Then he made a summary of their key points and produced a clear strategy that combined their ideas and his into three simple points (offer). Then he reconnected by asking them, "What do you take from this meeting that will fire us all up on Saturday?" (ask) and was showered with their decisions, both personal and for the group as a whole. He agreed to send them all a summary of the meeting via a cell phone message, and he ended with a sharp switch to a fixing style by asking for volunteers to come over and simulate the details of their agreed strategy. Then he instructed them to go straight out to the field to practice it.

Marco had a quiet way about him, but beneath his charisma was skill and experience in using MI to help athletes motivate themselves and take ownership of decisions, rather than having him impose solutions on them. The athletes spent most of the time listening to each other, and the more they shared their ideas, under his guidance, the clearer things became. Teamwork was happening inside the room.

Team Talks and "One-at-a-Time" Discussion

Can meetings, even brief ones like at half-time in a match, ensure *everyone* has a voice? A technique you might find useful is what we call the "one-at-a-time" discussion, where people sit around and give everyone time to talk. In Zulu it's called an *indaba,* and the method is widely used in education and other settings. It provides a near failsafe way of achieving the goals of both strategies described in this and the previous chapter, that is, giving athletes a chance to say what they think and feel (Step 1, Chapter 11) and helping them make decisions as a unit (Step 2 in this chapter).

Anna Experiments with Smart Halftime Team Talks

On the day we caught up with Anna, the coach of a college field hockey team, she used the "one-at-a-time" technique in a brief halftime team talk to make sure everybody got a say, and being experienced with MI, to make sure that they talked about why or how they might improve. She elicited change talk about the second half from them. Did she have the time? And surely she had messages she wanted to convey herself. "Sometimes" she said, "but you will be surprised how fast it goes once they get the hang of it. The challenge for me is to control my urge to solve the problem. I usually get a few moments to convey my message anyway."

Anna told us that she started this journey a few months back by just asking the players at halftime an open question like "What can we do to improve in the second half?" However, this took her out of her comfort zone because a few players dominated the discussion, sometimes openly disagreeing with each other when they only had a few minutes to talk. That's when she thought of using the "one-at-a-time" technique, which they had been using to good effect in longer game reviews or strategy meetings. The essence of it is to ask a question that everyone gets a chance to answer without any interrupting or cutting across each other. It's like a shortcut to MI because if that question is about change or improvement, they all express change talk. Box 12.2 summarizes what's involved.

The "one-at-a-time" method is most widely used in sports in longer meetings such as a match or competition review. Outside of sports it comes from efforts to resolve conflict or difficult decisions, where all relevant parties are gathered and everyone gets a chance to address a number of questions. For example, relevant questions in sports might include "What happened?"; "What do I think and feel about the match/competition?"; "What help do I need from the team to be my best?"; and "What help can I offer the team so we work better as a unit?" In the above example, Anna simply asked one question: "What can we do to improve in the second half?" She got lots of heartfelt ideas because the team was well briefed in the principles of this approach. Her summary and parting message was simple and clear, and it embraced some of the group's key messages.

BOX 12.2. MI and the "One-at-a-Time" Method

What?

A question is raised and athletes answer it, in turn, one by one. There might be more than one round, each one fed with a different question. Each person in the group gets a chance to answer the question, though no one has to speak if he or she doesn't want to, and an opportunity is left at the end for you to summarize. Most of the time in this process, people are listening to each other, and to you.

How?

Allow one round for each question. Pose the question; then hand over the conversation to the first athlete to answer it. When that athlete is finished, he or she then passes the task to the next one, and so on until everyone has spoken. You then summarize at the end. Some groups use an object like a ball or baton for the speaker, who passes it on when they have finished speaking.

Among the guidelines used most frequently are be positive, speak for yourself (not others) about how you feel, focus on the achievable and avoid blaming others, simply pass on the baton if you don't feel like talking, and no interrupting or cross talk, that is, only the person holding the baton may speak.

Applications

In halftime team talks, you have time for only one question, one round. In longer meetings there is time for two to three rounds or more, depending on the size of the group. The summary can be done by you or even one of the athletes.

Using Small Groups: A Discussion about Values

It's a powerful experience to agree on team or group values, to move beyond wall-mounted slogans, and the benefits are endless for teamwork. This is what Jim did in his role as a senior coach in a large swimming club. He says young swimmers can express values with ease and suggests that the earlier you encourage them to do this, the better. The idea was to do this exercise at the beginning of the year, because it then takes just a few seconds in a later gathering to remind them of those values. It's as if they are using their own shorthand language for success.

Jim was reasonably familiar with the principles of MI and had a very keen eye for using pairs and small groups to ensure that the discussion was safe, fun, and likely to ensure that athletes spoke about positive change. He preferred

> The benefits of agreeing on team values are endless.

working in smaller-size groups to make sure that everyone got a hearing and a chance to answer specific questions. When it came to values, he said this: "If the leadership of a club like ours, a really big one, can agree on these club values, then I can walk a straight line down to the level of an age group team and raise this subject, because I know that these values are more or less universal."

Here's how Jim addressed values, taking just 30 minutes or less. He gathered a group of 25 age group swimmers, many working in relay teams, told them what the purpose was, and asked each of them to give the group a statement about how each felt about coming down that day. The task was to throw a ball to whoever felt like speaking. That was the connecting warm-up exercise. Then he asked them to break up into pairs. Each young athlete was asked to take a minute to complete the sentence "My ideal swimming club would be like this: _____," and then switch around and listen to their partner complete the same sentence. Then he asked them to form small groups of five, and go around, much as in the "one-at-a-time" process described above, completing this sentence: "The strongest thing I heard being said was this: _____." Finally, in the large group he asked the swimmers to complete this sentence: "Teamwork in this club means _____," using the ball-throwing task to act as a link between speakers. The top four or five points apparently mapped well onto the values agreed by the club management, but not completely. So Jim took the exceptions into the next management meeting for their consideration. In this way, Jim noted, shared values started to become part of the DNA of the club.

Any sport can adopt an exercise like the one Jim used. It may be with quarterbacks and wide receivers, pitchers and catchers, or groups of attackers and defenders. The subject could be strategy, personal strengths, or struggles with motivation. The obvious value of small groups is that people get more time to talk. Also, in general, you will find it easier and more productive if you give players a specific question to address, allowing them to say what they think and feel and to make decisions, if necessary.

CONCLUSION

Cohesiveness and unity can so easily be eroded by the normal chaos that surrounds the organization and delivery of sporting performance. Even if you are not proficient at using MI, there are ways of maximizing equal contributions to decision making.

Using MI to improve relationships in a team or squad builds unity "from the inside." The greater their opportunity to express themselves and be involved in making decisions, the more likely athletes will act in accordance with those decisions. This logic drives the use of MI with individuals and in groups.

QUESTIONS TO CONSIDER

- How often do you let a group of athletes make a decision as a unit?
- What's the easiest decision you could allow your players to make together? How will you guide them in doing this?
- How skilled do you feel at being able to summarize a team discussion as a way of keeping it moving forward?

CHAPTER 13

Changing Behavior and Lifestyle

We need to do a better job of putting ourselves higher on our own "to do" list.

—MICHELLE OBAMA

HIGHLIGHTS

+ *Strategy:* Mapping priorities: What change? Use a mapping task to help athletes say for themselves how they might create better balance in their lives.

+ *Strategy:* Pros and cons: Why change? Help athletes to motivate themselves to make a change in lifestyle.

+ *Strategy:* Just ask! Connect, ask permission, and use MI to help athletes explore lifestyle change.

THE KICKOFF

Do you know that feeling of hesitation when pulling an athlete to one side to "have a word" about some aspect of his or her behavior or lifestyle? It's as if you know the reception might not be that great. This scenario gave birth to MI, in the search for a more a constructive route through difficult conversations about habits and lifestyle change.

Lifestyle balance can be a challenge for anyone. Athletes commonly struggle with meeting the need to do well in sports, to keep up with studies, and to make time to enjoy friends and manage home life too. It's a personal matter, and it is not always easy to talk about, which can make it difficult to make decisions related to one's allocation of time and attention to these

167

activities and to associated lifestyle habits such as diet, drinking, sleeping, and use of the Internet. What can seem a small adjustment to us might feel different to the athlete. The transition out of a sport is rightly being given

Athletes struggle with balancing sports and the rest of their lives.

considerable priority in many settings. Whatever the scenario, a conversation about change can be a challenge, and is often focused on behavior change.

FROM THE FRONTLINE

The coaching team had their targets and noticed something that kept reappearing each week: Jenny was overweight. They told her so and suggested she weigh herself in the gym and record the data so they could all help her address the problem. She never followed the advice. She felt restricted by all the "dos and don'ts" in her sporting life, as though there were no route to stress relief for her. The occasional big meal was one of her methods for dealing with stress. Then conversations got difficult. One day before practice, a coach took the direct route and told her straight, "You have great potential, we've invested a lot in you, and your weight problem needs to be tackled or your future is in doubt." The next day she decided to quit the team. Good intentions for a promising athlete took a turn for the worse. What seemed to count here is not just the problem the coaches saw but also how it was dealt with. MI was developed precisely for this purpose, to raise a tough topic and deal with it constructively. Instead of pushing for change, you come alongside, connect, share your observations, and encourage the athlete to find a way through. Better outcomes will be there for the taking.

You find these questions about lifestyle balance in every corner of sports:

> "He's a wonderful player, but I think he gets bored at home and probably snacks too much, and he's not able or willing to make a change."
> "She doesn't seem to think about transition out of our sport."
> "He is a good kid, but he hangs out with the wrong crowd."
> "Why would he throw it all away and get arrested again?"
> "It's those late nights, and she needs to watch it because it affects her performance. I told her that her sleep needs to improve."
> "Money in his pocket, and guess what? It looks to me like cell phone obsession, gambling addiction, and one very distracted athlete. Now it has to be addressed."
> "It's one thing to have some fun, another to get drunk so often. There's a problem developing there, and who knows how we will tackle it."
> "This young woman is clearly losing a grip on her studies."

No one is perfect. We as coaches can see a problem, but how do players see it? This chapter will clarify how MI might help you deal with athlete issues, whether via a brief conversation or through a quiet and more focused discussion. Put simply, your role is not to be the expert in an athlete's change but rather to have the tools to help them become the experts themselves; you help them to understand what is going on and make plans to achieve a better balance, or to make decisions about their future. Any person can point out what players are doing wrong in their lives. A skilled coach can help players have the courage to make lasting changes.

Choosing a *Strategy*

Your starting point to connect with a person should be in a style that is nonconfrontational. Upon this foundation we lay out a choice of three strategies (see below). They do not need to be followed to the letter; they are more like guidelines for making good progress:

- If the athlete will benefit from taking a step back to look at all the different elements of lifestyle change or future adjustment, then the *mapping priorities* strategy will be helpful. Moreover, if you want to raise a potentially delicate subject that the athlete could feel defensive about, then this strategy is ideal; through connecting with his or her lifestyle as a whole, it will be easier to raise a difficult topic, for example, secret gambling or alcohol use.
- If the topic to talk about is clear to both parties, but you suspect the athlete's motivation to change is low, then the *pros and cons* strategy is well suited to letting the athlete rather than you make the case for change.
- Maybe there is no obstacle to talking about lifestyle change, in which case you might *just ask* about it, which is described in the third and last strategy below.

STRATEGY: MAPPING PRIORITIES

Summary: Use a map to help an athlete sift through and make choices about the most important areas for change.

What change might best help an athlete to find better balance? For example, is it exercise or diet, both, or something else? Is it signing up for a course or looking for work? If you want to step back and conduct a review of an athlete's lifestyle and activities, then this mapping of priorities will help you do just that. The strategy is now widely used in health care and other settings (Gobat et al., 2018; Miller & Rollnick, 2012), and you could find it useful in your sporting conversations too. It's about exploring and agreeing on a clear way ahead and holds the promise of better outcomes than if the athletes were simply told they must or should change.

The challenge is this: There are often multiple and competing priorities that knock an athlete out of balance. The solution is to step back, look at the big picture, map out the priorities, and make smart plans together. Figure 13.1 illustrates what the strategy looks like; it's an example in which you actually use a piece of paper to construct a map. The strategy can easily be employed without pen and paper; it's just a matter of getting used to the tasks involved. We use the example of lifestyle change in this chapter, although the strategy is clearly useful too for discussion about the transition out of a sport.

Step 1: Construct a Map

• *Your task:* Introduce the strategy ("Can we step back and look at the challenges you face?"). You might even write down some of the priorities, using circles with words inside them for each one, as in Figure 13.1. Leave one circle blank for a topic chosen by the athlete.

• *The athlete's task:* Ask the athlete to comment on the priorities for change that you have identified and identify new ones if he or she can think of any (blank circle).

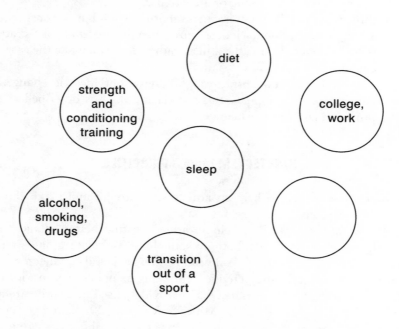

FIGURE 13.1. A map for setting priorities.

Step 2: Ask about Routes to Improvement

• Highlight and point to *possible* areas for improvement using questions like "What do you think about all these parts of your lifestyle?"; "Which area could you make an improvement in?"; "Have I missed any (pointing to blank circle)?"; and "I wonder about improvement here [pointing to one of the topics], but what do you think?" Notice how your use of "might" and "I wonder" steers you away from being authoritarian and rigid, helping the athlete to relax with freedom to say what he or she thinks.

• Steer the conversation toward decisions that the athlete *might* make. He or she might be ready to go for it and construct an action plan in one area, or perhaps not. At least you have started the conversation with this mapping of priorities and sown the seeds for further constructive conversation in the future.

Consider this example, where a coach and athlete are talking about the stress an athlete is under, and about how hard it is to find a balance in lifestyle.

COACH: You've given me a pretty clear picture of what you are dealing with at the moment, but can we get a little closer to what to focus on first and perhaps put a plan together? [introducing mapping]

ATHLETE: Yes, sure. It's a bit overwhelming at the moment. I'm not getting anywhere.

COACH: Of the three areas we looked at—diet, training, and academic work—which is going to be the most manageable and perhaps the most helpful for us to focus on? [mapping out the possibilities]

ATHLETE: Well, I guess it has to be my diet and how I eat; that's the thing I should have more control over. [choosing an option—change talk]

COACH: That might be useful for us to focus on in the first instance. [listening statement in response to change talk]

ATHLETE: Well, that would be good if we can put a plan together to help me manage how I eat; it's really important I get that right. [more change talk]

COACH: What's achievable for you right now, in terms of your diet? [open question about planning with a motivated athlete]

This isn't the end of the conversation but rather an important stage before constructing an action plan. Nevertheless, without this agreed agenda and the focus it provides, we wouldn't have the foundation we need for moving ahead into something like action planning.

When It's Hard to Even Raise the Subject

That example above was easy enough, and the athlete readily responded with change talk. It's not always so straightforward. People can get tied in knots when some part of their lifestyle becomes so problematic, they don't want to talk about it, and you are not sure how to even raise the subject. We have used the mapping strategy in some tight corners, such as with an athlete who developed a secret gambling problem that grew and became obvious to others. We used the mapping strategy to introduce the range of normal lifestyle behaviors that affect most athletes, and included the topic of gambling into this overview, just as one example among others. The athlete looked defensive and sad, and acknowledged that he was involved with gambling. Using this strategy in this way allowed us to gently ask how gambling was affecting his well-being. The door opened, and a journey began. Someone like a counselor might have been helpful in this conversation (see Box 13.1), but lifestyle is a normal subject not beyond the skills of friends, coaches, and even parents to talk about.

STRATEGY: PROS AND CONS OF CHANGE

Summary: Ask athletes to describe for themselves the pros and cons of a particular lifestyle behavior or decision they are facing. This allows them to sift through the options and see a more healthy and balanced way to proceed.

If there is hesitation or uncertainty about a change, then discussing pros and cons will help athletes come to a resolution. This strategy involves connecting, raising the subject of drinking, diet, training, schoolwork, transition out of a sport, or whatever. Instead of falling into a persuasion trap, you give athletes a chance to examine the pros and cons for themselves.

Here's an example with drinking alcohol as the focus. We assume you have approached the athlete, connected, and asked permission "to have a chat about your drinking."

> COACH: You clearly enjoy your drinking like many of the other guys, but what is it like for you, what do you enjoy about it? [asking about the pros]
>
> ATHLETE: Oh, it's just like the others, yeah; you get to let your hair down, and for me I like that it means I don't have to think about baseball all the time.
>
> COACH: Relaxing is important to you, and drinking has been part of that. [listening statement]

ATHLETE: Hey, it's not like I go home to a picnic, man—I get stress there too, so I got to get out of the house as well.

COACH: And maybe alcohol is part of how you deal with the stress. [guess in the form of a listening statement]

ATHLETE: You got it, Coach, but everything is OK, man, if you are worried about the way I drink . . .

COACH: I was gonna ask you, what's the downside of drinking as you see it? [asking about the cons]

ATHLETE: Downside?

COACH: Yeah, things you maybe don't like so much about the way you drink.

ATHLETE: Well, you know when you make those, like, joking comments at me about waking up on the practice ground—if it's early morning, I know I had too much of a heavy night the night before, that's for sure, and this affects my playing. [change talk]

COACH: You get a feeling of hangover, yeah, and what else? What else do you maybe not like so much about your drinking? (*The athlete mentions he is more likely to want to fight if he's had a drink— more change talk—and then the coach summarizes.*) So, let me summarize for us. It helps to relax and unwind, and it also gives you a hangover that maybe affects your playing, and you have to be careful about not getting into fights too.

ATHLETE: Yeah, you got it, Coach.

COACH: Where does that leave you with your drinking? What do you think is best? [open question that invites the athlete to clarify a decision about change]

ATHLETE: Less, Boss. I had better stay in a couple of more nights a week and cut back that way. [stronger change talk—a decision to change]

COACH: You can see how cutting back on drinking might work for you. [change talk]

Have a frank and connected conversation, free of judgment, and give people a choice—and they often do what's best for them. Asking about the positives first helps to cement connection and shows that you don't just view the behavior as a negative issue but also as a question of balance. Here's a summary of what's involved in asking about the pros and cons of change:

Step 1: Ask about the Positive Side (the Pros)

Keep a curious, nonjudgmental attitude, and ask questions like "How do you see the benefits of your drinking? What does it do for you?" Listen, make listening statements, and consider asking about other benefits.

Step 2: Ask about the Negative Side (the Cons)

Turn to the other side, and ask a question like "How do you see the downside of your drinking?" Take a little time here to explore a range of possible reasons drinking is not so helpful, and notice the lifting language that emerges. The athlete is saying why change might be a good idea. This language might be hesitant, it might be just a hint, but it's the start of acknowledging that there might be a problem.

Step 3: Summarize and Ask "What Next?"

This is a critical moment. The athlete has the answer about change and much of the motivation inside them. Trust it. Summarize the pros and cons as briefly as you can, not passing judgment but simply listing the key pros and cons, using "you feel" and "you," rather than "I," as much as you can.

Then ask a question like "I wonder what is next for you?" or "What do you think you will do about this?" Here's when a decision to change might emerge, and if not, you have a solid platform of understanding to take things a step further later if you so choose.

STRATEGY: JUST ASK!

Summary: A simple and direct route to using MI to address behavior change is just to ask athletes how they feel about a particular change. This opens the door for them to say why and how this might come about.

Our third strategy in this chapter sounds simple, and it is: Just ask athletes how they feel about a particular change, and use MI to keep a keen eye on the change talk as it emerges (see Chapter 3). The athletes will take ownership of adjustments they themselves have told you about.

> Just ask how they feel about making a change.

As any athlete will tell us, simple things often take practice and so it is with MI, which involves connecting first, clarifying how the athlete feels, and then pointing the conversation toward change. You will probably want to avoid potentially confrontational questions like "How come you didn't make it to training last week?" or "We need to do something about your diet, so can you come in to be weighed every week please?" Connect first (see Chapter 8), or you might plunge the athlete into defensiveness and resistance right away.

Here's a short conversation with a young athlete who is missing practice and under pressure. Instead of the opening being one of a challenge and disagreement, how about opening with an effort to connect and appreciate the pressure the athlete is under.

COACH: I notice that maybe with school pressures you didn't make it into practice last week. How's it going for you? [open question]

ATHLETE: Yeah, I've got so much going on with school and exams coming up.

COACH: Sports needs to take a back seat for a while. [listening statement]

ATHLETE: No, not necessarily, [change talk] but my parents want me to play less and focus more on school.

COACH: So, you want to keep involved and yet your parents see it differently. [listening statement, like a short summary of the dilemma]

ATHLETE: Yes, but I really want to do both. [strong change talk]

COACH: So, we need to find a way of managing the potential conflict in a way that all parties can be happy. [listening statement]

ATHLETE: Yes, exactly, and I'm determined to do both. [very strong change talk]

COACH: How so? What can we do to make that happen? [shifting conversation toward an action plan]

It took around a minute to connect, and you can now hear an appreciation of the dilemma. Taking that stance resulted in less of a battle and more acceptance and willingness from the athlete to begin to think about his role in planning and putting a strategy in place to satisfy the athlete's and his parent's potentially different aims. What may follow this brief interaction is an exploration of what the athlete feels they might do and what the plan would look like. More than that, it encourages him to take responsibility and take the lead in developing the plan—with the support of the coach and parents.

Questions That Call for Change Talk

You can probably come up with many suitable questions, but here are a few we find particularly useful:

"How might you find a better balance between school and sports?"
"How do you see the benefits of drinking a bit less?" (See the pros and
    cons strategy above.)
"What concerns do you have about making that transition out of your
    sport?"
"How might a change in diet help you in and outside of competition?"

Let the Conversation Unfold

Here's how that conversation above about sports–work balance might unfold. The athlete's motivation to change grew through the conversation. Now it's time to make an action plan.

COACH: How might you find a better balance between school and
    sports? [open question, invitation to make an action plan]

ATHLETE: Well, I have never really had this problem before because my
    school stuff has never been this important before.

COACH: You've always been able to put sports first; this is the first
    time you are having to take a lead on managing two different
    things. [listening statement]

ATHLETE: Yes, exactly, and I want to do both. [change talk]

COACH: What would the ideal plan look like in order to get the bal-
    ance right?

ATHLETE: Well, I guess there are a few things I could do. [change talk]

COACH: Tell me more.

ATHLETE: I can't do my work and my sport together, and my mom gets
    on my back about the work.

COACH: It's not easy, but you try. [affirmation]

ATHLETE: Maybe I can miss a practice session each week, just so I can
    catch up. [change talk]

COACH: That could be a plan; let's talk after practice and see what we
    come up with.

Using a combination of open questions and listening statements, this conversation is keeping the challenge with school and sports in the forefront but in a manner that encourages the athlete to begin to unpack what he needs to do and how he might do it. It may take additional conversations between the athlete and coach after the session, but it saves a huge amount of time in the long run and reduces the risk of losing the athlete completely.

TRANSITION OUT OF SPORTS

If attention inside a club is too narrowly focused on sports itself, then athletes of any age and in any stage of their sporting careers can find it hard to consider life beyond, even though they know that injury, poor form, not being selected, or outside pressures can prematurely launch them into the potentially unsafe world of finding a new career path and lifestyle. Many clubs and athlete organizations try to fill this gap by providing athletes with people they can speak to about life beyond sports.

Even a superficial reading of this book will highlight the conclusion that the best way to address transition out of sports is to talk about it within it, routinely, and well before the transition itself. A club where coaches and all involved realize this and commit to "having the conversation" is an obvious starting point, as is our often-repeated call to treat athletes like people first, athletes second. Then it is a question of how sometimes very personal conversations are conducted, and this is what the current chapter has been focused on. Normal conversations will produce normal outcomes for most athletes. MI skills can help you to have these.

ADDICTION AND MENTAL HEALTH PROBLEMS

Sometimes lives can get so seriously out of balance that the pain of getting through the day takes athletes into problems like addiction or the result of their suffering leads to panic attacks, agoraphobia, and depression. One common trap they fall into, that catches them out, is this: They have dreamed and dreamed about what they *want*, often succeeding against tremendous odds, and left behind is any understanding of what they *need*. Here's a good example.

FROM THE FRONTLINE

We recently had the privilege of meeting an elite sportsman with a pedigree of success that has his name still talked about decades after he retired. He told us that it could have been very different: He knew what he wanted, dreamed of success as a soccer player, and reached his dream with a contract with a top club. Sadly, his needs got left behind. In desperation, at age 19, he made a final decision to give up his sport and return home from the club where he was playing. The isolation was "killing" him, and he sank into depression. He missed his family terribly. Then, as if by sheer coincidence, his coach approached him, put his arm around his shoulder, and gave him cash to return home for the weekend with a promise to reconnect the next week. They did reconnect on his return, their conversations continued, and slowly the athlete's well-being returned. Both coach and player became household names and lifelong friends.

Every page of this book points to the value of having conversations that are caring because they focus on an athlete's needs—they inevitably improve human connection and outcomes. Yet all too often, in the absence of connection, athletes are left to fend for themselves, and small problems get bigger. Isolation can be a killer of an athlete's spirit. Those who feel unable to cope well with stress and isolation can develop addiction or other mental health problems. If you are friendly and approachable, and your conversations are routinely respectful of athletes, you may know about their lifestyle and home life to some degree. With such a relationship established, you will feel more confident to raise a concern when you notice it. Put bluntly, simple acts of caring can help to nip small problems in the bud before they fester and overwhelm the athlete.

If you feel that a problem you notice is too much for you to tackle, it is sometimes a good idea to help the athlete receive specialist mental health attention. Box 13.1 provides our best guidelines for good practice in doing this.

YOUR BALANCE

Whether you are the coach or the athlete, balance is an important part of your personal and sporting life. So many people work tremendously hard in sports, whether voluntarily or paid, and balance is undermined as a result. Ambivalence about your workload and other lifestyle challenges can unnecessarily drag on over time, and we hope this chapter allows you to reflect and even take yourself through some of the strategies described above.

Coaches also juggle competing demands. The stigma attached to struggling with mental health or addiction issues, as so many of us do, is one that need not drag us down. By offering an opportunity to have a conversation about managing (potentially) conflicting demands, you can help the athlete better manage the process of recovering. The tools we have described here should ease the process and give you more confidence to raise the issue of lifestyle conflicts.

BOX 13.1. Helping an Athlete through Addiction and Mental Illness

---

- Don't "dump" athletes with problems on a specialist. Keep the connection going throughout, seeing them on a journey toward better balance. You don't have to be an expert in mental health to continue to demonstrate care and interest in how athletes are progressing with their off-the-field challenges.
- Be sensitive about sharing with colleagues what athletes have told you about their private lives.
- Going for help is often a big challenge for athletes. Raise the subject only when your connection is well established, and make sure to give the athlete "something to think about," rather than using language like "you must seek help now." Be patient and reinforce freedom of choice.
- Be clear about your club's guidelines for handling mental health issues. Confidentiality is important and helpful for athletes to be reassured about. If you decide to break confidentiality because you are so concerned, inform the athlete first.

QUESTIONS TO CONSIDER

- You notice young athletes focused on their phones. How might you speak to a group of them about this, or to an individual?
- How comfortable do you feel about talking with athletes about their personal lifestyle habits? How often do you do this?
- You notice an athlete who seems troubled and down. What would it take for you to say that you notice this and want the athlete to feel free to chat about how he or she feels?
- Do you need to increase the amount of time you spend observing athletes?

CHAPTER 14

Coaching in Poor Communities

with Rob Maitra

I've seen it all around me in the ghetto: If you care as a coach, it lifts young people to heights they never knew about.
—DANIELLE COLON, senior, Hyde Leadership Charter School, Bronx, New York

---

HIGHLIGHTS

+ Athletes from poorer communities see their sport as way to reach their dreams, yet they carry weights that can't be ignored.
+ Using MI skills to keep connected over time allows you to address challenges more effectively.
+ A coach is not the same as a brother, sister, or parent. Keep your boundaries clear as you offer support and guidance.

THE KICKOFF

Sport looms large in poor communities. Biggie Smalls, in his song "Things Done Changed," raps, "Either you're slingin' crack rock or you got a wicked jump shot." Whether it's basketball players from streets of Biggie's

---

Rob Maitra, MA, is director of student engagement at New Visions Charter High School for Humanities IV in Rockaway Park, Queens, New York, and is a little league coach at Far Rockaway RBI (Reviving Baseball in Inner Cities). Previously, Maitra was dean at Hyde Charter High School in the Bronx, New York, where he was also varsity baseball coach. He has completed his coursework for his doctorate in cultural studies and education. He studied MI at the Health Education and Training Institute in Maine and joined MINT in 2016.

neighborhood in Brooklyn, soccer players from favelas of Brazil, or baseball players from the barrios of the Dominican Republic, young people can imagine sports as a path to success, wealth, and fame, a way out of the neighborhood, poverty, and obscurity. Everyday life involves higher rates of trauma, violence, classism, and structural racism. Sports brings together these hopes, dreams, and fantasies of success and respectability with poverty's challenges and obstacles, which can make coaching in poorer communities particularly challenging and rewarding.

Coaches come to this setting from all walks of life, not just because they know how much sports and exercise prepares young people for the challenges that await them, but also because of the sheer joy of observing them rising above it all, together. Against great obstacles, in neighborhoods that need this the most, sports can be an opportunity for youth to develop meaningful relationships with peers and adults and develop their self-esteem and agency. Just to get a team together, start a club, or get your hands on some gear is an achievement to be proud of, in defiance of a society that so often favors those with higher income and better access to facilities. Then the conversations begin, the games unfold, and you face some choices about how you can help young people reach their potential. That's where MI might help because it is not just about them being free of troubles for a while when playing sports but also about helping young athletes learn about life and themselves and deal with their challenges through sports. It's as if they carry a backpack that all too often weighs them down.

FROM THE FRONTLINE

He was a decent student at school, and as a wide receiver he was the star of the team and indeed the entire high school league. A loving and permissive grandmother raised him, and he struggled with all kinds of authority. As his coach, I figured out how to work not just *around* the problem but also *with* it: MI worked its way into many conversations, and he relied on me in times of trouble as he progressed through the high school. Then he got a scholarship to college, and we more or less failed to prepare him, to anticipate how he might deal with a more authoritarian coach who takes a traditional tough approach to sporting success. He didn't cope well, became isolated in a world where he was not the star of the team, dropped out, and now has a part-time job and gets high a lot. The college lost a talented player and a smart student.

—R. M.

Imagine that backpack which contains the challenges young athletes from poor communities carry as they enter the club, squad, or team. The higher the needs of the community are, the heavier the weight they will have on their backs, and this can include not just the impacts of a difficult childhood and threatening streets but also high expectations that are hard to fulfill.

FROM THE FRONTLINE

Jordan is a good example: He's one short step from going to jail, and his temper is a problem, holding him back in life and sports, and yet he's really good at baseball. It's a longer story, or put another way, his backpack is full and he's heading for trouble.

So many coaches in community sports have great love and affection for their athletes, and they feel like shaking their youth when they are at the precipices of life and saying, "Hold back. Just do what I tell you to do—listen to me. I know—I've made it through college . . . this can ruin your future." And so often this approach and use of the righting reflex doesn't work because the youths already know of the dangers and are feeling stuck. It's not that they don't know better, or need more information, but rather that they are ambivalent about the choice, about their future. It's not as easy for them as it might appear.

Working through MI with athletes from low-resource, high-need communities helps you to be less judgmental and more tolerant of the players' values, community, and culture; it also helps you to not get lost in overempathizing with athletes and using the righting reflex to rescue them. Rather, MI provides you with a compass to help them get unstuck and search for paths to achieve success, inside and outside of sports. In turn, that can be as rewarding for you as it is for them.

MI AS A ROADMAP

This work can feel like a juggling act where the highs and lows for the young people (and you) leave you wondering what your job really is. These athletes cannot simply avoid difficult situations, because they live in them, and you cannot help coming up against the impact of social, family, and economic stressors.

FROM THE FRONTLINE

When I first met her at age 10, I spotted two things: a passion for sports and outbursts that upset her and others. They lived in government housing; her mother had mental health issues and lost custody of her children for a time. I took time with her, and her skills improved dramatically; as she got bigger and stronger, she became one of the best players in the league. It was as if she felt shame in the face of failure. I spent time with her family to offer support and help her with balancing her emotions. There were good times when she "kept it together," and she used her will and skills to prevail, yet there were bad times too. If the team started playing poorly or losing, she could bring negative energy to the game. If she was pitching and another student made an error, she could get angry and yell at her ("Why do you even play softball?") or the coach ("Take her out of the game!"). There were meltdowns, stomping off the field, and always apologetic texts afterward. During big games, I would think to myself, *Today she will destroy one team on the field, them or us.* She made it all the way to the top of her game and then quit one afternoon when we lost in a playoff game. We still talk and text, and she says she has retired from sports and just wants to find a way to make enough of a living to survive.

MI was helpful with her because I had the skills to connect and learned over time to switch styles from fixing to following and guiding as the need arose. I tried never to judge her or make her feel bad. MI helped me to offer compassion and to never forget this question: "How can you use your skills to get better in life and sports?" That was my map, searching for the answers within her. I noticed other teammates learning too, about controlling their emotions and using the safety net I offered to them.

—R. M.

Put simply, MI helps you to see the person, not just an athlete, and to see through labels (e.g., problem behavior) and work with athletes' strengths, using sports as a gateway to growth in which your role is to encourage learning, not just ensure compliance.

While using MI calls for a more personal approach to coaching, this does not mean abandoning other coaching tasks where you take the lead in organizing activities; it's a question of balance and a call from our side to shift between coaching styles with greater flexibility (see Chapter 2).

THE WEIGHTS THEY CARRY

Young people in poorer communities often find themselves in or close to serious problems where things go wrong pretty quickly. They can become court involved without behaving differently from most teenagers. It's not just about "not going looking for trouble" or even that trouble finds them; it's that they live in a world of trouble. Hanging out with gang members or drug dealers might also be Christmas dinner or a christening celebration with the family, or a neighborhood BBQ. Here are some of the challenges that arise in and around the sports field:

Trust

Many athletes have difficulty in trusting adults, including coaches, especially those from different racial, ethnic, and socioeconomic backgrounds.

Implications for Coaching

Humility is a quality not often associated with coaching, and yet it's essential for building trust over time, along with patience and consistency. In addition to your knowledge about sports, you also need to listen and learn about the experiences and lives of the athletes. It becomes a two-way learning experience, a partnership. You use MI to work with the wisdom from the players, to help them find the change in themselves.

> Building trust takes humility, patience, and curiosity.

Unstable Anchors

Young people often feel they have an unstable anchor, having been up against hurtful and unpredictable experiences connected to challenges with housing, immigration, courts, domestic violence, foster care, financial con-concerns, or neighborhood violence. Their behavior is more erratic and explosive, while also making it harder for them to express themselves in words.

Implications for Coaching

With youth in poor communities, you may need to invest more time to create a sense of safety than with middle-class athletes. Work on creating a team culture that champions concern for others, support, and love. Your use of MI helps them to be more open about how they feel, with you and others, and this improves relationships and the culture itself. Anything you can do to foster stable relationships will help. As a coach you are a good listener and curious about your players. Help them to say what they think and feel as events unfold on and off the field. Consider building foundations through team dinners, home visits, and frequent and consistent communication in person and through texts, notes, regular team meetings (circles), and individual meetings.

Defiance and Fighting Back

The use of MI highlights what happens to athletes when verbally confronted—they kick back—and urban youth will often slip into fighting back, being defiant, or withdrawing into an angry state, which can exacerbate tension in a team and lead to power struggles. It's one thing to be clear about what is acceptable or desirable—being authoritative; it's quite another to use an aggressive manner in doing this—being authoritarian. Enjoyment of and success in sports (and life) involves a healthy expression of a wider range of emotions than just aggression.

Implications for Coaching

Roll with athletes' resistance by coming alongside and helping them to say what they really feel. MI helps coaches understand the potential of a partnership and how to strengthen and build a productive relationship. This also means avoiding the assumption that all wisdom and expertise sits inside you because you want to build their wisdom too. It also means being restrained with a confrontational style because this will limit athletes' reactions to defensiveness and aggression. The more you confront, the more resistance you will get.

The Dream Fantasy

Many young people invest everything they have in their sport, become deeply connected to their athletic self-image, and see their sport as their one chance at real success, fame, or respectability. Although they know, deep down, that they probably won't "go pro," the dream is the only one, and they are less confident about a "Plan B" that includes a good job, learning a trade, or going to college.

Around the field they can focus on their talent through effort, and working hard can be seen as a negative—they want to see themselves, and want others to see them, as naturally talented. Then if they lose, their willingness to learn from mistakes is low, and if a time comes for them to leave the team or sport, the negative shadow of failure can hit them hard.

Implications for Coaching

Talk with them about their needs and lives outside of sports. Focus on building their self-esteem and steps they might take to develop a "Plan B." Affirmation (see Chapter 5) is a powerful and simple way of building self-esteem. Elicit examples of people of similar backgrounds (class/ethnicity) and people from their neighborhood who have achieved success in other fields. Within sports, affirm and praise effort over achievement or talent, as effort will help them with their athletics and that Plan B.

> Talk with players about their lives.

Asking for Help

A successful athlete we know once looked back on his career and said, "Thanks for your help. I realize now that I never asked for help because we were taught not to before we could barely talk—it's like begging." Athletes might not ask for help when they most need it and can often refuse it when offered.

Implications for Coaching

Using MI to improve your relationship will enable you to choose the right moment to look forward and ask a question like "What help might you need to. . . . " It takes a little patience to overcome pride.

Focusing

The experience of struggling to focus is far more likely to affect an athlete who has been up against a host of challenges back home, noticeable in a range of behaviors such as looking distracted, agitated, irritable, or withdrawn.

Implications for Coaching

It's only by observing and connecting with athletes that you can grasp why and how players might struggle with attention. Some will appreciate an MI-led conversation about this very issue, which can give rise to simple, practical ideas such as being able to step away from practice because they are consumed by bigger life challenges, or using three to four deep, slow breaths to help them feel more settled. A consistent icebreaker or warm-up routine often helps with transition into practice or competition.

Parents

Parents under economic stress often have less capacity and miss out on supporting their children's participation in sports.

Implications for Coaching

Take opportunities to use all MI skills with parents, to initially connect and then to look forward, curious about what might help them become more involved. It might be difficult for them to find the time or transportation.

Host parent nights or breakfasts where they are specifically invited to attend. These conversations often strengthen the parent-child connection.

Trauma

Many student athletes have had serious trauma in their lives, sometimes called adverse childhood experiences (ACEs), and out of it have developed an overactive fight-or-flight (or freeze) response, or are suffering from post-traumatic stress disorder. They may respond to stressful situations violently (getting in fights during games or practice), give up, quit the team, or let anger overwhelm them, which negatively affects play. They experience shame when making mistakes.

Implications for Coaching

Help them to develop resilience through promoting strong bonds between teammates and coaches, and provide opportunities for players to experience success and achievement in the sport and in school and life. Consider mindfulness/breathing exercises to help them feel more in control, and help them to get counseling if they want this.

It is not all plain sailing for athletes when you use MI. They have probably spent lots of time with authoritarian coaches, and their first reaction might be to view an MI-influenced coach as weak or soft and not to be respected. They need the time and space to adjust and to realize that one can be caring and firm at the same time. Then there's the impact of this shift on you, which is what we turn to next.

YOUR WELL-BEING

There are inevitable choices you make about how involved you become in the lives of athletes, why, and what coping strategies you use to maintain your own well-being. What might start off as a well-intentioned desire to "make a difference" can become unhealthy and unhelpful. If you choose to listen with compassion to your athletes, rather than rely on a more authoritarian style, this in itself makes demands on your well-being. You can become overly involved, perhaps crossing what you know is a professional boundary. Using MI does not mean submerging yourself in their pain and problems, but you connect and help them face and overcome obstacles in their way. You can only really help people if you look after yourself and are modest and humble about what you can achieve.

Keeping to Your Boundaries as a Coach

A coach is not the same as a brother, sister, or parent. The boundaries can blur quite quickly when you step in to help athletes in poor communities, and you end up thinking things like "This kid is like a little brother to me" or "I feel like his father." Athletes themselves can also be heard to say things to coaches like "You're like a mother to me," often because they lack a role model at home. The danger here is that not only can this overidentification lead to burnout from the seemingly never-ending need to provide support of all kinds, but also being a parent, for example, is a long-term commitment, with complications in ruptured families that reach way beyond the confines of the sporting field, club, or team. As an experienced coach once told us, "If you are going to step in as a father, be ready to go all the way, or you will only let the young person down." Blurring the boundaries can lead to unanticipated outcomes. This isn't to say you can't show care or even a parental love for a young person, only that it's important to have clear expectations about the time and nature of the presence you will have in their lives.

For many coaches this conflict resembles the ambivalence or uncertainty conflict we discussed in Chapter 3: "I want to be of real help, but I can't be available all the time," or "I need to go to her house and talk straight about the problem, but I am not her mother." Consider clarifying this dilemma by asking yourself questions like "I feel like his older brother when . . . " and "I am not like his older brother when. . . ." Thinking deeply about what it means to be a coach can help to strengthen the boundary and keep you resilient. Talking with athletes about your role will also help, so they too get to understand what you are willing to give and what you are not.

Using MI should help to solidify and expand your role as a coach because you forge a partnership with the athletes and, while strengthening their autonomy, increase the impact you have on their decisions and life. There are times when you might be "brotherly" or "fatherly" without losing your central role as a coach.

> Clarify what it means to you to be a coach.

What You Take Home

Coaches often lead more comfortable lives than their athletes do. What happens when you open your heart to the challenges faced in poorer communities and you arrive back home? This can feel like a subtler form of coming back from war, where the hopelessness, trauma, and stress come home with you. That might sound extreme, but it does carry a warning to make sure you don't overstep what is an acceptable threshold or capacity for you when doing this kind of work.

As a caring coach, you have to let some things go. It's unproductive and sometimes damaging if a coach develops what's been called a savior complex. Humility goes out of the window, and the coaches believe they need to save the young people, when in truth our contributions usually have a much more modest effect. In any event the spirit of MI is to avoid seeing only the problems and to work with the strengths of athletes.

REAPING THE REWARDS

Working in an underserved community can be for many coaches a remarkably enriching, inspiring, and enlightening experience. What you get in return from your efforts with your athletes can be transformative—it might cause you to wonder who got more out of this relationship.

QUESTIONS TO CONSIDER

- You want to talk to an athlete who gets angry and upset very quickly. You know she faces hardship at home. What would be your guidelines for getting the best out of this conversation?

- The older brother of an athlete tells you they have been evicted and wonders whether you could write a letter to support their search for a house. You agree to meet them after practice in a café. What messages will you give them about your role?

- An athlete is confident and talented but hangs back in practice because, the athlete says, "I don't really need to practice that hard—I can do it on the day, no problem." How could you mess up the conversation?

CHAPTER 15

Connecting and Culture Change

> I am a member of the team, and I rely on the team.
> I defer to it and sacrifice for it, because the team,
> not the individual, is the ultimate champion.
> —MIA HAMM, professional soccer player

HIGHLIGHTS

+ More connection in relationships positively affects well-being, teamwork, sporting performance, and the culture of a team or club.
+ MI provides a concrete set of tools for improving relationships.

THE KICKOFF

We opened Part II with a suggestion from the journalist and ex-Olympic athlete Matthew Syed that it is more productive to connect well with athletes as people and to avoid treating them "like manual labourers, expected to listen and obey" (Syed, 2016). We then invited you to add MI to your coaching toolbox, to work within your relationships to draw out the wisdom and motivation to improve that sits within the athletes. By all means give them solid advice, but do this on the back of a respectful relationship. Focus your efforts intensely on winning, but do so by helping athletes to search for solutions themselves. As a colleague put it, when using MI, "I guide, they decide."[1]

---

[1] With thanks to Rick Reyes.

This final chapter lifts the lid on something bigger than conversations with athletes: how these connections between people are linked to motivation all around, and the wider atmosphere and culture in your team or club. What you place value on will affect all you do, for better or worse. How important is it for a club to value solid relationships?

FROM THE FRONTLINE: A LEADER'S CALL

The sport is baseball, but it could be any other, at whatever level. At the start of his time with the Chicago Cubs baseball team, CEO Theo Epstein shared with his staff a vision, which went like this:

> If we can't find the next technological breakthrough, well maybe we can be better than anyone else with how we treat our players and how we connect with players and the relationships with them. . . . Maybe our environment will be the best in the game, maybe our vibe will be the best in the game, maybe our players will be the loosest and maybe they'll have the most fun and maybe they'll care the most. It's impossible to quantify. (Verducci, 2017, p. 99)

The Chicago Cubs' culture changed under Epstein, a story we will return to, and the Cubs won the World Series in 2016 (108 years after their last World Series victory). For now, however, who exactly is the "we" Epstein is talking about? Certainly he means leaders like himself who guide the whole operation, and he also highlights the relationships between athletes. He no doubt also knew that coaches were central, so he hired a head coach, Joe Madden, who shared his values and had the luxury of wiping the slate clean and developing a culture in which people care for and about each other.

You might well be wondering how a web of interconnected and caring conversations can make such a difference to the culture of a team. We submit that at the center of creating a caring and winning team is attitude: the way in which your values and approach to coaching effectively guide not just how you speak but what you do as well, day in and day out.

> At the center of creating a caring and winning team is attitude.

This wide impact of attitude can be positive or negative. Consider some research on rude and disrespectful behavior, not that uncommon in sports, about how this behavior can seep into a group like a toxic virus, with serious consequences.

FROM THE FRONTLINE: RUDENESS SPREADS LIKE A DISEASE

People copy each other, particularly those more senior than them. For example, children who observe an adult abusing a doll will tend to do likewise. Supervisors who feel mistreated pass on this behavior to those they manage (May, 2015). Then consider this experiment: Twenty-four medical teams attending an educational workshop were given a simulated task, to diagnose and make treatment decisions about the plight of a newborn infant (Riskin et al., 2015). The stakes were high—the condition was potentially fatal. The experimenters designed the session so that teams were randomly assigned to receive one of two kinds of feedback from an outside expert in another country. One half received frankly rude feedback, such as they "wouldn't last a week" in his department, while the other half received feedback that was neutral in tone. The impact on decision making was remarkable: Teams exposed to rude feedback not only struggled to co-operate effectively but also were more likely to forget instructions, misdiagnose the problem, ask for the wrong medicines, and even mix the medicines incorrectly.

The relevance of these findings to sports is not hard to spot: Does shouting and yelling at athletes and making them fearful depress performance in both coaches and athletes? Put another way, might respectful conversations all round improve performance? We highlighted in Chapter 1 what psychologist Carol Dweck calls a growth "mindset" approach to your coaching (Dweck, 2017), in which, instead of focusing only on successful outcomes, you develop good relationships and thereby encourage athletes to take risks and even fail, knowing that the really powerful changes and improvements happen when athletes use the support you provide to reach their own conclusions about what went wrong and learn from their mistakes. What works the best is generally to affirm effort to the task, which is the aspect of performance that athletes have the most control of. This model is very compatible with MI. You focus on the learning process, not just the outcome.

CHOICES FOR COACHES

The choice about how you behave with those around you no doubt depends on why you want to be a coach. What gets you up in the morning? If it's only to win at all cost regardless of the well-being of the athletes, then much of this book will run against the grain for you. But look at the journey made by those Chicago Cubs, who were known locally as the "loveable losers" and were thought to be under the "Curse of the Billy Goat," for more than a century, until a change in culture and a focus on improving relationships launched a remarkable turnaround.

What gets you up in the morning?

FROM THE FRONTLINE: BACK TO THE CHICAGO CUBS

We spoke with Josh Lifrak, the head of mental conditioning at the Cubs, and he confirmed the account of coach Joe Madden's arrival in the team and the impact he had. Madden's golden rule was "Connect, trust and lead—in that order" (Verducci, 2017). Lifrak described how before Madden arrived with that message from the top, they had conducted interviews and conversations from the "bottom up" with young players and parents about what it really meant to be part of their team. Madden listened to these reports, and an agreement was forged about the principles that were to guide this fresh start for the team. The number 1 rule was "Make a personal connection first; everything else follows." He met with managers, coaches, and players and said, "We need to get to know each other. We need to start trusting each other. And then we have to start bouncing ideas off one another without any pushback" (Verducci, 2017, p. 214). This was clearly not just talk. Madden lived this approach on and around the field of play, and the players grew into this way of being with each other. That phrase, "without any pushback," captures the goal of MI (see Chapter 6 on rolling with resistance): to have skillful conversations that go beyond arguing, blaming, and always being right, to searching for improvement with humility, curiosity, and respect for one another. That describes MI in a nutshell. The attitude of respect and trust goes both ways, from coach to athlete, from athlete to coach, and between players too. This attitude grows and affects coaching technique itself. For example, Lifrak recalled how the coaching staff tried to avoid telling players that they were wrong because "the moment you start saying 'that's wrong,' they get defensive and you lose collaboration" (Josh Lifrak, personal communication, 2018). By placing an emphasis on building relationships, their organization's performance improved all round.

You have a lot of options, wide latitude to work out how you want to be with athletes. Yet the starting point, a genuine desire to connect, respect, and communicate with skill, is a simple one. Starting with that desire leads to choices about how to proceed and contribute to improving the culture. You might mull over these questions as you think about the culture you want to promote in your team:

- Why did you go into this work?
- What excites you about this job?
- What are your assets as a coach?
- Where could you improve?
- How is your behavior consistent with the answers to the questions above?

CHOICES FOR ATHLETES

In this book we have championed the use of MI to give athletes freedom to grow, make decisions about their own improvement, and learn to fit in and fly with their teammates. High ideals maybe, but then we are reminded of the simple courage of those young tennis players in a ghetto when one of their teammates was killed by a car on her way to the camp. Their coach gave them choices about what to do, and they found a way. It wasn't that complicated; MI guided the spoken word, respect for choice drove the conversation, and the athletes rose to the occasion. If athlete empowerment sounds too touchy-feely for sports, consider this example of players making choices together in the heat of battle.

FROM THE FRONTLINE: THE CUBS REBOUND

Tom Verducci's account of the last game of the 2016 World Series, viewed as the most anticipated game in baseball history, highlights the remarkable role of player relationship, in this case in the face of impending disaster. It was the final inning of Game 7, and the Chicago Cubs had given away a healthy lead. The rain came down to force a delay, and the players walked off the field, "their heads dropped and their faces blank . . . [with] the look of a team that knew something bad had happened to it" (Verducci, 2017, p. 345). How might they relaunch themselves with renewed vigor and clarity of purpose?

One of the drivers of recovery was a risk taken by first baseman Anthony Rizzo just before the start of the earlier do-or-die Game 5, when the Cubs were also staring at defeat. They needed to win the last three games in a row to take the World Series. Rizzo did a naked dance in what was described as "an inspirational and comedic presentation" (Verducci, 2017, p. 320). The scene went wrong when another player sprayed an aerosol over Rizzo, whereupon he disappeared into the shower. When he reappeared, his close friend Ross comforted and inspired him with the words "It's not how many times you get knocked down, it's how many times you get up . . . ," whereupon Rizzo rose up and repeated his naked dance. They won Game 5, so Rizzo repeated his ritual before Game 6, which they also won, and then again before the final Game 7.

At that critical rain break, a request was made for a player-only meeting in which they shared encouraging appeals to their motivation and self-belief. A different team came out to face the music. In the dugout with Rizzo due to bat soon, his friend Ross shouted to him, "It's not how many times you get knocked down . . . ," to which Rizzo replied, "It's how many times you get up. . . ." Everyone laughed. They won the game, and with that, as Verducci noted, the culture had been redefined (Verducci, 2017, p. 363). Something close to 5 million people attended the victory parade in Chicago.

The Cubs players were channeling the words of one of the world's most transformative leaders, Nelson Mandela, who said, "Do not judge me for my successes, judge me by how many times I fell down and got back up again." In the Cubs' journey to undo the curse, and in Mandela's words, lies the heart of MI. We succeed by empowering people to get back up in the face of challenges. We succeed by working to transform the team culture to support them to get back up.

The culture of a team is different when athletes make choices for themselves, guided behind the scenes by supportive coaches. Like the effort to produce a spectacular musical or stage play, what goes on in the act itself takes months of expert planning and belief in the ability of the performers to produce the goods when it matters. The Cubs' coaches had mastered the art of guiding athletes to be at their best when it mattered—and realized the MI mantra "I guide, you decide."

Consider the words of one of the most successful coaches, Anna Botha, coach to Wayde van Niekerk, 400-meter Olympic champion sprinter and world record holder: "I try to handle them as human beings with feelings, emotions and to guide them not only on the track but in everyday life. My main goal is that when they leave my coaching, they leave as respectful, balanced and lovable people" (Dennehy, 2017).

QUESTIONS TO CONSIDER

- How would you describe the culture of your team? Is the atmosphere friendly, cutthroat, collaborative, depressing, competitive, or trusting?
- If you were having coffee with a colleague and she asked you what your most important goal was for the athletes you work with, what would you say?
- What are the two to three most important things you could do to make the atmosphere in your team friendlier?

PART IV

MI PLAYBOOK

In this part of the book you will find quick-reference sheets for learning about and applying MI. These sheets cover topics that stand out as signposts to improving your everyday conversations and outcomes with athletes, which in turn can lift a team's culture.

Specifically, these sheets cover the following:

1. Coaching Mastery: A Guide for Parents, Fellow Coaches, and Support Staff
2. Relationships: The Foundation of Masterful Coaching
3. Empathy: Becoming a Better Coach
4. Overview of Motivational Interviewing
5. MI Mindset
6. Learning MI
7. Useful Questions
8. Listening: Getting the Basics Right
9. Summaries
10. Teamwork 1: Improving Social Skills
11. Teamwork 2: Making Decisions as a Unit

Coaching Mastery:
A Guide for Parents, Fellow Coaches, and Support Staff

You might be in the car on the way home, in the locker room, or on the side of the playing field. You might be a parent or a coach, or in any other role in the team.

Things might have gone well, or not well. You have a moment to be helpful. Here are some guidelines:

The Philosophy

- Sport is important, but life as a whole is more important.
- People first, athletes second.
- Fun, first, and foremost.
- Connect first.
- Advice without connection can be harmful.

Mistakes and Getting Better

- When athletes feel upset or frustrated, give them time and support to recover.
- Learning happens best when they feel connected and calm.
- Making mistakes is how people learn.
- Trust them to learn from mistakes.
- What the athlete notices from a mistake is more important than what you notice.

Motivational Interviewing

- Be in the right mindset to speak to an athlete.
- Connect and empathize with how athletes feel.
- Ask them before telling them.
- Notice and highlight strengths.
- Listen while they tell you why and how they might improve.
- Summarize the positive things they tell you.
- Ask them what the next step might be and what a good plan might look like.

Skillful Coaching

- Coaching is a skill set.
- It takes time, courage, and humility to be a good coach.
- You never arrive at destination "good coach." The journey never ends.
- Enjoyment and connecting are infectious and lead to happier outcomes.

SHEET 2. Relationships: The Foundation of Masterful Coaching

Good relationships in sports don't just happen but are worked on and built up, and if they are undermined, they can be repaired. They do not cost any money, athletes thrive on them, and they correlate with well-being, higher motivation, better teamwork, and improved performance. Poor relationships demotivate athletes and can spread into the culture of a team like a virus.

Develop Trust

It is possible to work on building trust. Distrust brings the worst out of athletes. It makes it harder to motivate them, undermines self-confidence, and affects performance. Developing trust is not about being weak, soft, or losing control of decisions.

- Be *reliable*—follow through on decisions.
- Be *consistent, caring,* and *honest*.
- Be *transparent*—avoid talking about athletes behind their backs.
- Develop practice routines that focus on player cooperation.
- Communicate—show interest in them as people, in their lives outside of sports.
- Listen to their concerns.
- Address problems by being clear and compassionate at the same time.

Show Respect

It's only by showing respect yourself that you earn it. Its absence undermines relationships and good progress, and can cross over into bullying, abuse, and harassment.

- Highlight respect as a core principle.
- Provide examples of what respect is, and what it isn't.
- Model respect for others in all you do and say.
- A key practice for modeling respect: listen.

Encourage Enjoyment

It will be easier to win when you and your players enjoy their sport.

- Look after your own well-being. Search for opportunities to enjoy yourself.
- Look for opportunities for players to have fun.
- Ask players for ideas for building fun into practice routines.

Express Empathy

This is a skill and the most direct route to building relationships, improving trust, and showing respect for athletes. It's a skill where you listen to athletes and tell them what your understanding is of what they are saying and experiencing.

- Before talking to athletes, imagine what they might be feeling and why.
- Ask them open questions about the issue, regardless of the subject.
- Convey your understanding through using listening statements and summaries.

Motivational Interviewing

MI uses a good relationship to help athletes to motivate themselves and make plans that make sense to them and you.

SHEET 3. Empathy: Becoming a Better Coach

Empathy is a talent we can develop through intentional practice, much like athletic ability. As you get better at empathizing, it not only affects the athlete and your conversations; it changes you.

What Empathy Isn't

Empathy isn't being friendly or kind or solving problems for athletes. It also isn't "feeling sorry" for athletes or pitying them.

What Is Empathy?

Empathy is standing in someone else's shoes, imagining their experience. You get to see how they see things, all the better for helping them to find the next step. You say something that shows them you are connected (empathy goes beyond something you feel).

What Are Empathic Listening Statements?

A technique for conveying empathy is empathic listening statements; you say something that captures their experience—a statement, not a question. They recognize that you are "with them," that you care and understand how they are feeling. This allows you to build powerful connections over time.

MI and Empathic Listening

In MI, you ask about improvement and use listening statements to help athletes dig deeper, resolve uncertainty, and firm up their plans.

Why Empathize?

Teachers with better empathy skills have students with higher grades. More empathic counselors have clients with better outcomes. Increasing your natural talent for empathy can make you a better coach, improve your life away from sports, and lead to better sporting outcomes.

The Technique

Listen in order to capture the meaning of what someone is saying. Then, give that meaning back to them in a statement. It might feel awkward and pointless at first, but the payoff comes just as surely. Here's how it looks:

ATHLETE: I'm fed up with my progress. I'm getting nowhere fast.

COACH: *You are not happy about this.*

ATHLETE: Say that again.

COACH: *Something's not right with your technique.*

ATHLETE: I think I need to. . . .

Conclusion

Practicing empathy is an essential counterbalance to the fixing skills that we use all the time in coaching. Using empathy does not oblige you to give up your passion for excellence. It also does not mean you must change your personality. Empathy will indicate you consider your athletes' perspectives to be valid, and thus give a "green light" to them to express whatever they are feeling. It also shows you are willing to listen and can respond without pushing. If you eventually decide to give advice (fix), athletes will be more open to your ideas once you have connected with them.

What Is MI?

Think of it as a coaching style, comprising communication tools and strategies for drawing out athletes' internal motivation for doing better, whether as individuals or in a team.

Main Message

Telling, commanding, and instructing, used exclusively, can lead to pushback, or even undermine athletes' enthusiasm. MI provides tools for engaging better and helping athletes to motivate themselves to address challenges and reach their potential.

History

New in sports, MI developed in behavioral science as a method for lifting motivation and encouraging behavior change.

The Coach's Attitude

Coaches use a mindset shift, from fixing to guiding—"I have ideas to offer you, but I am curious about how you see yourself improving." Trust and mutual respect are the foundation for this shift and for using MI.

The Method

The method consists of a defined set of communication skills, such as curious open questions, listening statements, affirmations, and summaries. These are used to draw out athletes' ideas about how they might improve on and off the field. The more coaches use these skills, the better the athletes' performance, self-confidence, social skills, and your relationship with them will be.

Focus on Language

As athletes talk about change, they use language that lifts their motivation. Your job is to notice this and encourage it.

Highlights

- You can connect skillfully and rapidly in most conversations.
- Structured strategies for lifting motivation can be learned and practiced.
- Advice or feedback can be delivered with listening at its center.
- Pausing and listening are powerful responses to argument, disappointment, or difficult behavior.
- Affirmation is a powerful alternative to praise.

What Is an MI Mindset?

In sports we are programed and trained to fix. We teach, advise, and correct. *Fixing* is a critical style needed by coaches, managers, and all involved with fitness, performance, diet, and well-being. A second style needed for coaching mastery is *following,* where you listen well and demonstrate empathy or understanding. Then a third style is *guiding,* on which the MI mindset is based: You actively and purposefully guide athletes to offer up what's important to them in their development. Having these three "speeds" requires practicing shifting from one to the other in conversations with athletes individually or in groups.

Main Message

All humans have a "righting reflex," a tendency to immediately jump in and correct something we see as wrong. There is wisdom in holding the righting reflex in check, "staying cool," and using the following and guiding styles from your toolbox.

The Coach's Attitude

One motto for MI in sports is "I guide, you decide." Making a decision to use a guiding style is the first step, but being an excellent guide takes practice. Learning skills that help you to be centered and relaxed in each conversation helps you to have better access to your MI skills, in the same way that a focused and prepared athlete will have better ability to perform.

The MI Mindset: Getting Better at Guiding

Breathe. Regulating your heart rate by breathing slowly for 1 minute (4 seconds in through your nose, 4 seconds out through your mouth) can help keep you to keep calm as a coach or athlete in sports and other settings. Take a couple deep breaths before you have an important conversation to help slow yourself down.

Self-Coach. Before a conversation that you know will be tense, remind yourself and the player of the purpose of the conversation—for example: "I want to start by simply listening to this player during the next few minutes," or "Jimmy, I would just like to take a few minutes to understand your perspective. How would you feel about that?" This commitment to yourself and to the player may help a great deal in staying focused and resisting the righting reflex.

Catch Yourself Fixing. It's never too late to turn your conversation around. At any point you notice your focus weakening, you can apologize to athletes and remind them (and yourself) of your hopes for finding what might be helpful to them—for example: "Hold on a second, Maria. I'm sorry—I got a little carried away there. It's just that I'm really passionate about helping you be at your best. Please tell me your point of view on this."

Once you have grasped the basics of MI, sort out for yourself where it fits into your development.

The Basics

Learning MI often starts with observing rather than stepping in, taking time to wonder about what will motivate an athlete. When you notice athletes not responding to your efforts, could you draw solutions and inspiration from them? Consider these routes to progress:

- Focus on those three communication styles (fixing, guiding, and following), and practice shifting among them.
- Catch yourself before acting on the *righting reflex,* and practice asking searching, open questions that you don't necessarily know the answer to.
- Practice using a guiding style with questions about improvement. Then produce listening statements by imagining athletes' experience and offering your listening statements back to them. Other skills from the toolbox (like summarizing and affirmation) soon become familiar means to move the conversation forward.

What's Your Priority?

Learning MI requires that you step back and observe yourself and the athlete in conversation. From that position of observing, you can then take whatever MI strategy makes sense to you and practice using it—for example:

- *If you are or want to be a good listener,* explore using listening statements efficiently, along with purposeful guiding questions. Summaries will help you to move on in a conversation and not meander.
- *If fixing is a harder habit to break than you expected,* just stepping back will reap rewards, and all the skills of MI are open to you.
- *If you enjoy the technical side,* you should notice immediate improvement when you use the "ask–offer–ask" strategy for providing advice and feedback.
- *If you tend to be a bit too serious,* remember that you don't have to solve every problem. Good guides also enjoy what they are doing, and they let the athletes do most of the work!

Practice

You learn MI the same way an athlete learns new skills. What's your next goal for improvement? Which athlete can you try things out with? Who will help you to improve your skills? Use MI with everyday coaching challenges. Jump in and try these skills. In the end, it's down to enjoying practice out there with athletes themselves.

SHEET 7. Useful Questions

Questions are a great way to get the best out of athletes, particularly if you invite them to search for answers with a guiding style and questions that are "open" rather than "closed." You might or might not know the answer yourself, but this is not so important—it's what the athlete uncovers that's important.

Use questions along with other skills, such as listening and summarizing. Notice evidence of strengths as they talk, and use affirmations to highlight these. Open, thoughtful questions can help you deepen your connection with athletes and can also be more focused on improvement.

To Connect

Curiosity is your number 1 starting point.

- How did you manage to hit that ball so hard?
- What happened for you out there?
- How is your game going at the moment?
- How are you today?
- What's it been like in practice today?

Ideally, use listening statements immediately after the athlete responds, and if you get a bit stuck, summarize and move on to another question.

To Address Improvement

When using MI, questions are forward-looking and designed to focus on improvement and change. The answers to them will be change talk, things that athletes say that help them to motivate themselves.

Behavior Problem

"How do see yourself dealing with this better in the future?"

"What are the benefits to you of handling this more constructively?"

"You are late for practice again today. What can you do to improve next time?"

Motivation

"What's going to help you get fired up today?"

"How do you see the benefits of moving to your new position?"

"How important is it for you to have an overpowering serve?"

"How confident do you feel about covering their left wing?"

Goal Setting

"What's holding you back?"

"What goal do you want to aim for?"

"Why is this goal important to you?"

"What will help you to be your best?"

"What's the best way for you to reach this goal?"

"How committed are you to this plan?"

"What's helped you in the past?"

"What's the first step you could take?"

MI involves using the skill of listening in a purposeful way when talking about improvement. To do this, it's important to get the basics right.

Listening reinforces your respect for the athlete's own wisdom, and your care for the athlete as a person. It entails hearing what is said and then responding in a way that demonstrates you are present (not distracted by other thoughts or pressures) and that you care. As is often the case, clearing your mind and following your curiosity will set you up to listen well.

An example: The day before a big competition, one of your top athletes says, "Can you sit down, because I have some really bad news." Your mind is immediately clear and receptive, and you are curious about what's going to be said. Connecting involves curiosity and only one focus: the athlete's experience or concern.

Hear what is being said: "Yesterday I was told that my brother's been taken to the hospital, and he's really close to me. They say he collapsed and had a heart attack, at 19 years old, and now he's in intensive care and two hundred miles away. He's alone, and maybe I need to go and see him, so now what?" Imagine her brother lying in a bed in an ICU.

Summarize it in your own mind: Read what the athlete in our example said; then turn your head away from this page and summarize for yourself what you have heard. Keep it brief. Here's our suggestion: "You've had quite a shock, and you are not sure what to do."

Say your summary back to the athlete: "You've had quite a shock, and you are not sure what to do." That's a listening statement. She will feel that you understand and quite naturally will want to say more.

Don't jump in: Stay quiet, pause, and even take a breath, because your statement is an invitation to her to speak more. Notice her reaction.

Being precise is not the goal: If you are genuinely curious and you don't get it quite right, the athlete will correct you—and if she doesn't, just ask her to. Your listening statement needs to be somewhere in the ballpark of correct, but it doesn't have to be a direct hit. As long as the athlete knows you are listening, you can expect the conversation to proceed productively.

Simple statements: Some listening statements say more or less what the athlete has said ("Your brother is alone and not well, and you want to see him").

Complex statements: Some listening statements are more complex, adding new meaning that you hope is accurate. They might speak to an underlying meaning or feeling that the athlete left unsaid ("You are not sure you can make the competition tomorrow").

Double-sided statements: Your statement might also capture both sides of a conflict or dilemma ("You might want to do the competition, but you need to see your brother").

Statements that focus on emotions: Or you might comment on the athlete's feelings ("You are really upset about him").

Questions and listening statements working together: If you start with a curious question, try to follow it with two to three listening statements. As you confirm the athlete's experience with the statements, the connection between you strengthens.

SHEET 9. **Summaries**

A summary is a striking opportunity to highlight both the strengths of the athlete and whatever has been said about change. Giving a summary can go wrong if you focus only on problems or deficiencies. Here are three brief summaries offered to an athlete, a hurdler, who has asked his coach for help with his form. They all involve accurate feedback, but notice the differences among them.

Summary of Deficits

"If I can just summarize, OK? [Pause.] You are struggling with your form, and you don't quite know why this is. Maybe your right arm is not quite right at that first jump. Or maybe you don't raise it quickly enough. You head out there and tend to overthink things and slip out of that zone, and you don't know how to get back into it."

Accurate: Yes.

Focus on a person with strengths: No. It's about an athlete with deficits.

Focus on change: No.

Summary of Strengths

"If I can just summarize, OK? [Pause and wait for athlete to indicate he is open to hearing the summary.] You've got your life outside of athletics in good balance right now. You have been determined to improve your times, and yet you are struggling to get back into that zone you know so well. You have worked hard at trying to figure out what's going on with that right arm."

Accurate: Yes.

Focus on a person with strengths: Yes.

Focus on change: No.

Summary of Strengths, Using MI

"If I can just summarize, OK? [Pause.] How to get back into that zone is not easy for you, yet it's something you are determined to deal with. It's a question of how. You don't want to overthink it all right now. You think there might be a way to change your right arm as you approach the first hurdle. You are going to try this out this afternoon."

Accurate: Yes.

Focus on a person with strengths: Yes.

Focus on change: Yes.

The first summary focused on problems. The second was focused on a person with strengths, contained a number of affirmations, and carried the potential to lift morale. Only the third, though, was consistent with MI—because it had forward momentum and effectively summarized the change talk that was heard. This last one is most likely to lift motivation and affect behavior change.

SHEET 10. **Teamwork 1: Improving Social Skills**

The first step in building teamwork is to help athletes improve their social skills. As they do this, they develop respect for each other, and teamwork improves. In short, you want the players to improve their skills at saying what they think and feel, listening to others, avoiding blaming others, interrupting less, and allowing quieter athletes to talk. Here's a quick sketch of how to do this.

Aim: *Open discussion* in which players say what they think and feel, free of fear.

Scenarios: Informal conversations and group meetings.

Getting started: The discussion can focus on any subject that they all have a view about. It could be personal or linked to sports. Help them to use the skills when talking about simple topics to begin with. When you feel more confident, try guiding them through using these skills in a discussion when strong feelings are around, such as after losing a competition or game.

Doing it right: You may need to kick off these group conversations at first. But keep the discussion among the players. Think of it as if you are tossing a balloon into the group with an open question, then stepping back as they toss the balloon around among themselves.

Guidelines to Be Shared with Athletes

- Respect for each other is essential.
- Speak for yourself and about how you feel, rather than about others.
- Listen rather than interrupt.
- Feel free to say nothing.
- Give space to the quieter ones to speak as well.
- Commit yourself to working on the issue as a team, together.

Coach Conduct

- Gently but firmly reiterate guidelines.
- Ask a positive, open question about something they have in common.
- Avoid interrupting, passing judgment, or solving problems.
- Use listening statements; capture what's been said and then hand the baton straight back to them to say more.
- If all goes quiet, consider questions like "What else?" or "What do others feel?"
- Summarize before moving on.

Traps

- Avoid back-and-forth conversations between you and individual athletes.
- Don't give advice or solve problems (yet!).

From *Coaching Athletes to Be Their Best: Motivational Interviewing in Sports* by Stephen Rollnick, Jonathan Fader, Jeff Breckon, and Theresa B. Moyers. Copyright © 2020 The Guilford Press. Permission to photocopy this material is granted to purchasers of this book for personal use or use with athletes (see copyright page for details). Purchasers can download enlarged versions of this material (see the box at the end of the table of contents).

Once you have guided your players in sharpening their basic social skills, in the second step to improving teamwork, you can now help them focus on making decisions together.

Aim: Help a group to make decisions together.

Scenarios: Small or large meetings, informal or formal.

Skills: Take the skills from Sheet 10 and refine them. You want athletes to listen to others, avoid criticizing others' ideas, and accept group decisions for the sake of the group.

Topics: Easier decisions first on any subject—personal or linked to sports.

Doing it right: Keep returning the floor to the players, such that they make the decision, not you.

Guidelines to Be Shared with Athletes

- Respect for each other is essential.
- Speak for yourself and about how you feel, rather than about others.
- Listen without interrupting.
- Feel free to say nothing.
- Give space to the quieter teammates.
- Go along with decisions that the majority agree on.

Coach Conduct

- Remind the players about guidelines.
- Ask a positive, open question that will unite their focus on the decision.
- Avoid interrupting, passing judgment, or solving problems.
- Use listening statements, which capture what's been said about the decision and which hand the baton straight back to them to say more.
- If all goes quiet, consider questions like "Who else would like to speak?"; "Where are we with this decision?"; "What else do you need to discuss?"; or "Who else feels like that?"
- Summarize their progress with the decision (and ideally the outcome agreed on). Adjust any part of the decision you feel you need to.

Traps

- Avoid back-and-forth conversations between you and individual athletes.
- Don't make the decision for them (rather, offer suggestions for them to decide on).

Useful Techniques

One-at-a-Time Technique: Here, you make sure everyone gets a chance to speak, and the athletes also get high-quality time listening to others. Each round involves answering one question. Ask them to address the question one at a time, in turn, briefly, without interruption and with freedom not to speak. Other guidelines: No cross talk; speak for yourself, not others; and say what you think and feel. This technique is excellent for resolving conflict and can be used very briefly, even at halftime in a match. More rounds and questions can be used with more time available.

Ask–Offer–Ask Strategy: When you want to contribute information or suggestions, (1) ask athletes what they know about it and listen well, (2) offer ideas as suggestions, and (3) ask them what they think about the decision you are making together as a unit.

Solo Tasks: Have players address a question privately, even writing down their thoughts.

Pairs: In turn, have them listen to each other's answers to that question. This method is good for very focused discussion.

Appendix

RESOURCES

For readers working in the sport world who are interested in deepening their MI knowledge and skills, here are some additional resources we would recommend:

BOOKS

For a Fuller Understanding of MI

Miller, W. R., & Rollnick, S. (2013). *Motivational interviewing: Helping people change* (3rd ed.). New York, NY: Guilford Press.

Teaching Yourself Manual on MI

Rosengren, D. B. (2018). *Building motivational interviewing skills: A practitioner workbook* (2nd ed.). New York, NY: Guilford Press.

Using MI for Your Own Personal Development

Zuckoff, A., & Gorscak, B. (2015). *Finding your way to change: How the power of motivational interviewing can reveal what you want and help you get there.* New York, NY: Guilford Press.

ARTICLES

Mack, R., Breckon, J., Butt, J., & Maynard, I. (2017). Exploring the understanding and application of motivational interviewing in applied sport psychology. *The Sport Psychologist, 31*(4), 396–409.

Markland, D., Ryan, R., Tobin, V., & Rollnick, S. (2005). Motivational interviewing and self-determination theory. *Journal of Social and Clinical Psychology, 24*(6), 811–831.

Vansteenkiste, M., & Sheldon, K. (2006). There's nothing more practical than a good theory: Integrating motivational interviewing and self-determination theory. *British Journal of Clincial Psychology, 45*(1), 63–82.

References

Beale, M. (2018). In the zone. Retrieved December 15, 2018, from *www.coaches-voice.com/rangers-coach-michael-beale-steven-gerrard-liverpool-chelsea*.

Clement, P. (2017). What would Carlo do? Retrieved November 11, 2018, from *www.coachesvoice.com/if-i-was-a-player-id-love-to-play-for-a-coach-like-him*.

Cohen, G. L., & Sherman, D. K. (2014). The psychology of change: Self-affirmation and social psychological intervention. *Annual Review of Psychology, 65,* 331–371.

Dennehy, C. (2017). Botha's recipe for coaching success: Patience, endurance and perseverance. Retrieved November 27, 2018, from *www.iaaf.org/news/feature/anna-botha-iaaf-coaching-achievement-award*.

Dweck, C. (2017). *Mindset-updated edition: Changing the way you think to fulfill your potential.* London: Hachette.

Egan, G. (2013). *The skilled helper: A problem-management and opportunity-development approach to helping.* New York, NY: Cengage.

Elberse, A. (2013). Ferguson's formula. Retrieved December 15, 2018, from *https://hbr.org/2013/10/fergusons-formula*.

Fordyce, T. (2017). Ashes: Inside story of England's 5–0 defeat in Australia in 2013–14. Retrieved October 12, 2018, from *www.bbc.co.uk/sport/cricket/41859201*.

Gillespie, J. (2015). Jonny Bairstow is good enough for the Ashes but be brave and back him. Retrieved December 17, 2018, from *www.theguardian.com/sport/blog/2015/jul/20/jason-gillespie-column-england-jonny-bairstow-talent-ashes-recall*.

Gobat, N., Copeland, L., Cannings-John, R., Robling, M., Carpenter, J., Cowley, L., . . . Moyers, T. (2018). "Focusing" in motivational interviewing: Development of a training tool for practitioners. *European Journal for Person Centred Healthcare, 6*(1), 37–49.

Hattie, J., & Timperley, H. (2007). The power of feedback. *Review of Educational Research, 77*(1), 81–112.

Kohn, A. (2001, September). Five reasons to stop saying "Good job"! Retrieved December 15, 2018, from *www.alfiekohn.org/article/five-reasons-stop-saying-good-job.*

May, C. (2015). Rude behavior spreads like a disease: Scientists study the contagion of obnoxiousness. Retrieved December 11, 2018, from *www.scientific-american.com/article/rude-behavior-spreads-like-a-disease.*

Miller, W. R., & Rollnick, S. (1992). *Motivational interviewing: Helping people change behavior.* New York, NY: Guilford Press.

Miller, W. R., & Rollnick, S. (2002). *Motivational interviewing: Preparing people for change* (2nd ed.). New York, NY: Guilford Press.

Miller, W. R., & Rollnick, S. (2012). *Motivational interviewing: Helping people change* (3rd ed.). New York, NY: Guilford Press.

Pascal, B. (1958). *Pascal's pensées.* New York, NY: Dutton. (Original work published 1670)

Riskin, A., Erez, A., Foulk, T. A., Kugelman, A., Gover, A., Shoris, I., . . . Bamberger, P. A. (2015). The impact of rudeness on medical team performance: A randomized trial. *Pediatrics, 136*(3), 487–495.

Rosengren, D. B. (2018). *Building motivational interviewing skills: A practitioner workbook.* New York, NY: Guilford Press.

Rowen, B. (2018). Chasing the "Holy Grail" of baseball performance: Inside the wide-ranging search—led by economists and psychologists—for the elixir that turns good squads into great ones. Retrieved December 11, 2018, from *www.theatlantic.com/magazine/archive/2018/07/finding-the-formula-for-team-chemistry/561722.*

Ryan, R. M., & Deci, E. L. (2000). Self-determination theory and the facilitation of intrinsic motivation, social development, and well-being. *American Psychologist, 55,* 68–78.

Sinek, S. (2011). *Start with the why: How great leaders inspire everyone to take action.* London: Portfolio.

Syed, M. (2016). Ranieri has achieved greatness with a measured approach. Retrieved December 11, 2018, from *www.thetimes.co.uk/article/matthew-syed-ranieri-has-achieved-greatness-with-a-measured-approach-pfz2nzmpl.*

Vaughan, J. (2017). Misguided praise junkies. Retrieved December 15, 2018, from *https://playerdevelopmentproject.com/misguided-praise-junkies.*

Verducci, T. (2017). *The Cubs way: The Zen of building the best team in baseball and breaking the curse.* New York, NY: Crown Archetype.

Wylleman, P., & Lavallee, D. (2004). A developmental perspective on transitions faced by athletes. In M. R. Weiss (Ed.), *Developmental sport and exercise psychology: A lifespan perspective* (pp. 503–523). Morgantown, WV: Fitness Information Technology.

Index

Note. *e*, *b*, *f*, or *t* following a page number indicates an exercise, box, figure, or table.